Praise for
My Female, My Male, My Self, and God . . .

"Anneliese Widman, a well-known New York psychotherapist, has given us an unusual and poetic spiritual autobiography. Her book will be an inspiration to all those who have struggled with the scars of early abuse and its attendant pain and confusion in adult life and relationship. As she movingly documents, it is only by patient reflection on the deeper spiritual meaning in our suffering and by finding a full and honest relationship with ourselves — both the dark and the light within us — that we can find peace and wholeness. A fine, courageous, and challenging book."

Roger J. Woolger, Ph.D.
Author, *Other Lives, Other Selves* and
The Goddess Within

"This work, written with the stark honesty necessary for therapeutic growth, stirs hidden truths in the reader's unconscious and bubbles them to the surface to be dealt with. Widman's vivid images and intense feelings are a powerful vehicle, stimulating memories useful on the path to wholeness . . . courageous . . . a model for other works in this genre."

Ronald Robbins, Ph.D.
Author, *Rhythmic Integration:*
Finding Wholeness on the Cycle of Change

"Dancing for Anneliese Widman, I felt her impatience with mere movement, with any hint of irony or cynicism. 'Show me your male, show me your female,' she entreated, 'show me the deepest aspects of your being.' Her dance, like her writing, is full-blooded, direct, and radiantly symbolic, a vision of the fearless self."

Douglas Dunn
Choreographer

My Female, My Male, My Self, and God

Anneliese Widman, Ph.D.

My Female, My Male, My Self, and God

A Modern Woman in Search of Her Soul

Anneliese Widman, Ph.D.

ANT HILL PRESS
GEORGETOWN, MASSACHUSETTS

North Star Publications
P.O. Box 10
Georgetown, MA 01833
(508) 352-9976 • fax (508) 352-5586
http://www.ReadersNdex.com/northstar

Cover Design: Salwen Studios, Keene, NH
Cover Art: Eric Holzman

The poems by Rumi on pages 1 and 163 were originally published by and are used with the kind permission of Threshold Books, 139 Main Street, Brattleboro, VT 05301.

Printed in the United States of America

Publisher's Cataloging in Publication
Widman, Anneliese.
    My female, my male, my self, and God : a modern woman in search of her soul / Anneliese Widman.
    p. cm.
    ISBN 0-9655067-0-3

    1. Widman, Anneliese. 2. Bioenergetics. 3. Psychotherapists—Biography. 4. Dancers—Biography. 5. Femininity (Psychology) 6. Masculinity (Psychology) 7. Dance—Psychological aspects.   I. Title.

QP517.B54W54 1997   574.19'121'092
                                                                QBI96-40823

Dedication

To all those who, in their own searching, have picked up this book and found their paths crossing mine.

Acknowledgments

To my parents:
Were you not who you were, the concept of *Reflectivism* would have remained unhelpfully buried in my psyche.

To Dr. Alexander Lowen:
Your teachings in Bioenergetics were necessary and invaluable starting points in my development.

To Dr. John Pierrakos:
Thank you for taking over my mentorship as I progressed from Dr. Lowen.

To Dr. Roger Woolger:
Thank you for taking me beyond the boundaries of finite psychology to see the limitless horizon of my spirit.

To Rev. Phyllis Woodbury:
You gave me tools which have led to the fruition of my concepts. For your belief in me always, I thank you.

To Alcott Allison, my editor:
Thank you for the extraordinary confidence you have shown in my work.

To George Trim, my publisher:
Thank you for your unusual and thoughtful assistance in bringing this book to publication.

Contents

PART THREE: The "I AM"

Foreword

What follows is a history — my history: from traumatized child, through the searching for healing from others, to comprehending my own healing through helping others to heal themselves by my work as a psychoanalyst. Along the way I have incorporated key principles from Bioenergetics in synthesizing a therapeutic approach that answers the spiritual longings and agonized cries I found neglected in my own journey.

Through this synthesis I have accepted and validated my pain. Only in doing so could I progress to the frightening, ultimate act of self-healing — accepting the responsibility for my pain by accepting its roots in my own nature.

In my soul's past I tapped the sources of my parents' cruelty. My present personality mirrors these wellsprings, the seemingly random abuse of my childhood, and explains my earlier obstinate self-sabotage of a wholesome, wholehearted relationship.

I call this synthesis "Reflectivism." In presenting a modality that goes beyond the conventional principles of Western therapy, it has seemed to me in keeping with the nature of my experience to offer my own journey as an illustration. In order to telescope a transformation of many years' length, as well as to express the fundamental spiritual basis of that transformation, I have chosen to tell my story in a format of poetic prose mingled with poetry — a synchronicity of vitality and meditation.

To tell my story I have learned that the pain one feels is always, and solely, the "reflection" of one's own inner turmoil, brought out into "objective" existence for detection, comprehension, and resolution.

I believe my story can help you to understand the process of self-healing, as encoded in Reflectivism. In all humility, I celebrate my own healed pain, as the means which led me to this place of helping to heal others . . . perhaps you as well. I hope so.

— Anneliese Widman, Ph.D.

The Question

Who am I, God?
Who am I, really?
I have not left a stone unturned
to find the balance that I seek.

The "not I" in which I was encased
left me like a blinded beggar.
The "I" that ensued was ever more conscious,
but I am still not balanced.

What is this restlessness
that pervades?
It is the whispering voice of the soul,
asking my psyche to awaken further.

Are you the voice that can help me fuse
the "not I" and the "I" to the "I am"?
Then take me in hand,
Thou masterful teacher.
Lead the way. I will follow.

There is more, there is more,
that much I know.
There is a fusion with another self.
They say it is higher than the "not I" and "I."
Lead the way. I will follow.

I cannot bear the state I am in,
that wishes to throw life away.
I cannot live without that beautiful balance
of a psyche that can say,
"This is who I am."

Many years ago, I read in the writings of the Hindu mystic Yogi Ramacharaka of three states of being: the "not I," the "I," and the "I am." I have borrowed these terms in my psychological work, convinced that Ramacharaka would find my tribute complementary to his original conception.

The "not I" state is one of psychic lostness, a defensive state: the soul, curled into a self-protective fetal position.

The "I" state is one of a consciousness that can perceive its reality. Yet, its day-to-day reality does not satisfy a yearning for connection, communion . . . with what, it can hardly say.

The "I am" state is that of "the higher self," "soul," the essence of being, the core.

Two words that can become three.
I am Anneliese. I, Anneliese, am.
Anneliese, I am.
They are round, they are whole,
they are rich, they are bountiful,
they are glorious.

They are here, they are there,
They are everywhere.
They are never nowhere.
They are I, they are me, they are you,
they are we; they are never not I,
nor me, nor you, nor we, nor not any of us,
nowhere.

I am woman, I am man, I am God.
So are you, so are we, so are they.
When we are not, and are lost,
we can reach and be found,
for we are surrounded by us everywhere.

We are truth, we are love, we are joy,
we are hope.
We believe, we have faith, we know,
that Thy Will being done,
not mine alone,
will bring us the right to our throne.

We live from this height,
our feet on the earth,
our heads soaring into the sky.
We have truly created a wholeness thereby,
that will connect us to our God.

I have divided my story into three parts, corresponding to my development through these states of being. The third state, the "I am," is an ongoing narrative. No end is in sight . . . only new adventures. And joy. Joy at my triumphant sense of interconnection. Joy at the peace I feel.

PART ONE

The "Not I"

Late, by myself, in the boat of myself,
no light and no land anywhere,
cloudcover thick. I try to stay
just above the surface, yet I'm already under
and living within the ocean.

— Rumi

1

The "Not I"

That utter darkness, that mass of protoplasm,
moving in space in semi-blindness, relating to
itself in idiotic fashion, succumbing to others
as though they were gods and goddesses,
amassing each year of life,
with an expectancy of change
that never happens.

This world is the world of the voices
contained in each of us,
depending on the onslaught
we were subject to from the beginning.
I have no "I" to buffer the hateful incoming energy.
I stagger with each blow like a punch-drunk boxer
in the ring, waiting for the bell
before the next round.

Round after round, I thrust out my arms
to ward off the Other.
The Other, sensing the nature of the thrusts,
their impotent, egoless strength,

quickly disposes of me.
I slink away into a corner of myself,
into a corner of the ring.

"You can do it," says my aide, "you can do it.
Get up. You can do it."
"I can," I mutter senselessly to myself.
"I can do it."
I shake my head to pull my consciousness
to another state.
It rises to the occasion, only to hear
the clank of its chains
slam the door to a possible new horizon.
Like a giant standing at the gates,
the voice reverberating from my brain, to my aura,
to the Other, shouting that I am only a powerless
mass that can be buffeted hither and yon by
anyone.

Thus I feint and parry with life, but seldom thrust
a blow into the body of life so I can shout
inwardly:
"Aha, I've got you this time!"
The voices become my ego.
I march to their rat-tat-tat discord
until I stagger,
mesmerized by their compelling power,
to hide in a rat-infested cave within my psyche.

This is the world of the "not I," a world in which
reality is perceived at a great distance,
a distance becoming more and more remote,
until the organism must will itself to stay alive.
Death would be too frightening;

and I inwardly know,
for choosing death defiantly
the curse of God would be upon me.

"Not I," think I. "Not I," say I.
"You are, but I am not.
I am not, but you are," think I, silently.
"Somewhere, I must be.
I'll try this. I'll try that.
I'll be like her; but as her, I am not.
Who cares?
It is being something, somebody, someone.
It feels like something, somebody, someone.
But my body aches with the burden of the
Other I carry around with me.
If I shed this burden, I will be lost.

"When will I allow myself
to be truly lost,
so I can be found?"

I was born in 1921 to a woman who, at the age of twenty, found herself pregnant. Mamma was born in an Alsatian village at the beginning of the twentieth century. She was the beauty of the village, with long, black hair she wore loosely in a bun at the nape of her neck. Her features were classic French: a long delicate nose, the nostrils flaring like a bellows when she was excited. She was vain, self-involved, energetic, and volatile.

Mamma was reared by a Prussian father, who ruled the family with true Prussian values: the kitchen, the children, the church. Her education did not continue beyond the age of fourteen, at which time she was trained as a jeweler. It was at this time that her mother died. A year later, she gained a kind stepmother, twenty years older than she. Mamma never mourned the loss of her mother, carrying her agonized tears inside her until her own death.

The atmosphere in the home was one of terror of doing or saying the wrong thing. The goals were to please the monarch, her father, and hide whatever secrets she had about anything personal. Since the siblings were at all times protecting themselves from the father's wrath and tyranny, it was a house of deceit and cruelty to one another. The young stepmother soon learned that she had married a monster. Since at that period there was no way out, she stoically maintained whatever vestige of self survived in her.

Often, she would come to the rescue of her stepchildren; all four of them would cringe in a corner of their home until the monarch's wrath was spent. They fearfully huddled together until he was satisfied with his powerful effect on them. He would then gently and cajolingly bring them one by one to his presence, where their secrets would be stealthily and cunningly pried from them. It was in this way that he learned about Mamma's pregnancy of three months.

It is dark, damp, and foul in
this tight dungeon.
There is no breath.
There is no warmth.
There is no feeling of being welcome.

She is astonished that I am here.
After three months,
she can no longer hide the bulge
I make against the walls of her uterus.

What is this sharp instrument that
enters my dungeon?
I'll move away from it.
I won't be cut out of this prison,
even though it is hideous in here.

I made a contract to be born to you,
loveless woman.
You are exactly the right
emotional dimension for my growth.
You do not want me?
You wish me to die?
I'll show you! I won't die!
You'll have me despite your loathing!

Oh, God, what is this contract I have made?
I need the strength to push my way out.
But she fights against my every movement.

Push, push, tear her to pieces, if need be.
Push your way out!
Don't let her succeed in killing you.
You have let others do that before.
Push!
Ram your way into the world.

Push!
It is time to be born!

Mamma had been wooed by a young man three years older than she. He also was a jeweler in their place of work. The young man was totally smitten by her beauty and, although she was not much enamored of him, he pursued her until she succumbed to him sexually. This sexual act became a fatal one, for it sealed her marriage to my father. Realizing that she was pregnant, she confided in her stepmother. Together they schemed and plotted about what to do. It was after one of the monarch's tirades that he, suspecting the situation, forced his young wife to tell him the dreaded secret.

The young man was called to the monarch's household and confronted. He consented to marry her and to take responsibility for the offspring. They married and lived in the young man's village, only a kilometer from the village of her own birth.

My father was the fourth in a family of five children. He was tall, dark in appearance, handsome, and extremely sensitive. He was a talented jeweler. He idolized his new wife. She, however, was discontented with her pregnancy, feeling ill throughout most of it. She needed to continue working because my papa was constantly hospitalized, treated for a shrapnel wound from World War I. This wound never fully healed, making his right leg infirm. Mamma worked grudgingly, as she had begrudged her pregnancy, as she begrudged her daily visits to her husband in the hospital. I was, nevertheless, born six months later in the midst of what could hardly be considered a honeymoon existence.

Two years after, Papa, finally declared well enough, decided to go to America, the land that would give them a better life. Post-war Germany was a country of poverty, unemployment, and political upheaval. All his siblings had preceded him to the land of opportunity, so he journeyed forth by himself, leaving his wife and child behind.

After a one-year trial period in America, he returned to Alsace, telling his family about the wonders of the new land. He stayed with us for two months, planning with Mamma the future move to a new home. It took him another three years to accumulate enough funds to bring us to the new continent. Finally, however, he came back from America to collect us. We left Germany and Europe behind.

We moved into a German neighborhood in New York City, gradually becoming part of the melting pot of America. Papa worked as a jeweler for a large firm, until many years later he started his own jewelry business. He was an adventurous man, a man of high principles, though fearful and delicate, a man always seeking to please his wife.

2

Mamma: The Female Energy

Mamma breastfed me for fifteen months, three months beyond the accepted time for the women in her village in Alsace. At the end of this period of time, she had to go to a sanitorium for extreme back pains. Of course you get pains in your back when you breastfeed your infant beyond the normal span of time, claimed the villagers. They looked upon her as a veritable martyr. I was weaned quickly and thrust into the arms of my paternal grandmother, who whispered from time to time into my ears that she loved me. This became indelibly imprinted on my psyche. Someone did love me. But not my mother.

> Mistress of hopelessness,
> despair is the word I coin from
> contact with your foul-smelling body,
> your icy stares, your corroded touch.
>
> Why did you have me
> if you did not relish me
> inside your stinking womb?
> Why do you place your nipple
> inside my eager mouth,
> when all I feel from you is

contempt, loathing, and the need
to prove your womanhood?

Your milk is sour, but I suck and suck
to stay alive,
so my destiny with you
can be fulfilled.

You push away these eager fingers
and call me "pig."
I freeze against your
pulling back my nourishment.

I can only wonder
how it would feel to fall asleep
against your breasts —
my cheeks so radiant and pink,
from that innate satisfaction
derived from the woman's substance.

I could have pulled yours into mine,
to grow like a healthy seed
emerging from a rich, strong earth.

3

Papa: The Male Energy

Papa was not around much, having gone to America when I was two years old. The male energy for me, therefore, was nebulous, lending itself to vagary and fantasy.

I remember a meeting with my father in a harbor, when I was three, upon his first return visit. I remember a large vessel coming to shore from a distance. As a three-year-old, I perceived the ship to be like a phantom coming out of a misty nowhere, having on board a giant figure whom I called "Papa," who would save me from the wrath of my mamma. As he approached me and Mamma, I curtsied to him as a "lady-in-waiting" might do with a monarch. The curtsey brought forth much laughter from him. Henceforth my heart was opened to him, bestowing upon him all my hopes, dreams, and expectations.

I recall being told about an incident that had occurred during infancy pertaining to my papa. The story made me wonder for the first time if this trip to Earth was one I could cope with. The incident was as follows:

My voracious and unyielding temperament made me howl when I was in need. I was told I would howl all night from the frustration of having the breasts taken away before my appetite was sated. My howls were shattering to those around, and one night my papa lost his patience. He hurled my fifteen-pound, screaming body against the wall, from which I rebounded, then I dropped into my crib. The violence silenced me and I became motionless.

I had a dream in which I was put on the back of a pony and taken to the heavens. There, my wounds, primarily on my head, were healed with ointments. I was given the choice to stay or to go back. I decided to return.

When I awakened in my crib and looked into the faces of my parents, I was changed. I had withdrawn and would no longer cry, scream, or make demands. I became instead a silent, passive observer.

Only a few months old, I had found a way to stay alive. My way was to contract my eyes, the optic thalamus or energy center in my forehead, so I could not focus clearly upon the world, which was essentially "them," my parents.

4

The Two Cellars

I remember an anecdote that operates remarkably on two levels: one, as a compelling and heartbreaking example of the destructive dynamics of my parents toward each other and me; and the other, what appeared to be a subconscious correlation of experience to the surface story.

Lotte, my mamma, jealous of the occasional demonstrative affection between my papa, Ernest, and me, had retaliated viciously by compelling her dominated husband to betray and humiliate me by upending my dinner plate on my head. After my night of sobbing, the next day unfolded as follows:

The next morning, Mamma shrieked at me to get out of bed. She charged back and forth with her daily duties. She looked in my direction and ordered me to do this and that. Papa sat and stole glances in my direction. No one spoke to me directly.

I did not know what I had done, but humiliation swept through my body. I wandered about, guilt-ridden, wondering whose pardon I should ask; or would it be best if I stopped existing? My eyes became glazed as I watched her frenzied activity.

I wondered about their contact with one another. There was no indication that anything was amiss. The drama of this household was in full swing. It never occurred to me until many years later that my parents' theatricality was anything but standard household behavior.

We ate breakfast and I sat, as usual, between the two of them. He stole a glance in my direction and offered me a piece of his roll, which he buttered first. At this gesture, she slammed down her coffee cup. He screamed at her "to get off his back." It was now she who was stunned. Realizing I would be her next victim, I quickly left the house, running all the way, whispering, singing to myself, "He loves me, he truly loves me. He is my papa. And he loves me. He truly loves me."

As I sang these words, I felt my body healing. The "not I" of my psyche began to stir, to crawl out of its cave, to look for crevices in the walls to which I might attach my fingertips and pull myself up and out, closer to the light, the air, to the fire of life, onto the bountiful earth on which I might be able to stand once again. My nature sang because I thought I was loved. Nothing in life was too difficult, not even my mother.

The male peers who taunted the girls could feel that day the strength, conviction, and power which emanated from my aura. They did not dare tease me or poke fun at me. I was Athena, the warrior goddess, loved by the gods. Was not my papa one of those gods? I breathed from head to foot. My cheeks blazed with health and vibrancy. "So am I truly," I thought at the well-being I experienced. "So am I me."

In my heady sense of being loved and invincible, I and my three-year-old friend decided to go to a cafe that entranced us with its cake, whipped cream, and hot chocolate. We ran with utter excitement, discussing our forthcoming feast.

The blood was coursing though our veins; our bodies were two pieces of fire as we ran to the cafe, when suddenly a giant hand clamped down upon my right upper arm. I felt myself being whirled around and pulled in the opposite direction. The pace was so fast I stumbled most of the way. As I became accustomed to that fierce grip upon my arm, I dared to look up, to recognize my papa, red in the face, frothing at the mouth, an unrecognizable monster. He said nothing. When we finally came into the vicinity of the house, I saw *her* standing, her arms folded, a look of glee that said most clearly: "Now we'll see who has the upper hand!"

He opened the cellar door and began pushing me down the steps. I had seized his middle finger and held onto it as tightly as I could so as not to be hurled into that dark, rat-infested place. No matter how I howled and shrieked, he would not stop. Slowly his finger slid away from me. It was the only grasp I had on life and reality.

When I reached the firmness of his fingernail, I felt life ebbing from me. I went back behind my eyes as I fell into the darkness, registering in my psyche before he slammed shut the cellar door a sinister yet gleeful smile on his face.

I sat motionless, my mouth ajar. It had been frozen in a terrified scream, no longer audible. My eyes had stiffened into the same expression. I do not recall how long I sat in this position. The information seems to be buried in my memory. It is a crazed feeling of stunned disbelief, of man's inhumanity to man.

Perhaps I fainted, perhaps I died. I know that parts of me did die. This experience broke some aspects of my spirit, which is what my parents wanted. I do not know nor recall when they opened the cellar door. I can reconstruct that they eventually opened the door and called to me to come out. I can reconstruct that I walked out into the light, dazed and forlorn. I can imagine that they might have screamed me into more reality because the sight that greeted them frightened them. I was beyond a "not I" state. There was no recall once the cellar door had been shut. What occurred is frozen into my psyche, unavailable except for some images that are vaguely familiar.

Another cellar comes to mind, a dungeon. The memory of it trickles faintly into my consciousness. As I coax the memory out of me, I see a dungeon, below the ground, its occupant an old, white-haired man, very frail. He is a scientist with unusual ideas, ahead of their time. He is being tortured and tormented. The torturers and the populace of the community want him to admit that his ideas are not valid and that he does not know what he is talking about. From time to time they come into the dungeon to stomp on his back, which has been broken many times. His shrieks are of no avail; they will not hear him. He is not normal, not of them, and his ideas disturb the population. They believe that which is different from them must be tormented until it dies.

The old man is silent, waiting for his suffering to be over. He pleads with the unknown deities for all to be finished. They also do not hear him. "Is there more I must learn about man's inhumanity to man?" he cries, looking into the heavens. "What more, God? Let me die now. I have no need to learn more."

He dies in time, for the body can finally take no more torment, nor can the soul keep the organism in existence beyond its endurance.

I wondered to myself how I knew about the scientist. I thought it was too coincidental, my having been put into a cellar in this life, then recalling a life of similar torture. In this life I have also experienced emotion concerning man's inhumanity to man. In this life I have been a terrified being, yet courageous, persevering with my destiny, searching endlessly for my real self.

"How do I know this?" I wondered. "Will the pieces ever come together? Will I finally be able to make sense of who I am? Why do I need to know about the whole? Why can't I be content like others with scattered fragments of information about myself?"

I now have another glimmer of understanding. I realize that I am doubtful about my own intuition because I hear my mother's voice inside me most of the time. Her voice is filled with skepticism and ridicule about my perceptions. She couldn't tolerate opinions different from hers. I'm beginning to understand how much I imbibed her fear and lack of curiosity. I scream out loud: "This is disgusting. Any resemblance to you disgusts me."

After the cellar incident, my spirit, though broken, was not destroyed. I looked at my papa with a faint smile. I told him with my eyes that he was forgiven. I was convinced that he would not have committed that terrible act if not for my mother. I let him know with shy glances behind my mother's back that I understood him as no one ever had, that I could look into his soul and see his goodness.

I was convinced I was right. This faith was my buoy and I clung to it tenaciously as I mobilized my strength to continue in that household.

5

Genital Development

I'm four.
My body speaks with a voice
that is strange to me.

There are bubbles,
pulsating, circular,
drunken bubbles,
circling around and around
my lower body.

Mamma says
this part is called a vagina.

I jump up and down
so the bubbles
will stop bubbling,
or be cast out of me.

I want to say to them,
"Leave me alone.
You're upsetting me.

You draw attention to yourselves
day and night."

It was so when my mother
boarded me out, while she
went to work.
No one was at home except
a woman in a wheelchair
who oversaw me.

She fell asleep, though,
and I felt the bubbles
ever more strongly.
I jumped up and down
to make them stop,
but they fizzed even more.

I wanted to rock my body
to and fro, but when I did,
their intensity increased to
such a point that I needed to
insert something, to quiet
the ever-increasing energy.

A poker!
Yes, the poker by
the fireplace.
It will stop the moving and stirring.
In it went, but I felt only pain.
I stopped because she, in the
wheelchair, awakened.
When she looked at me, she
screamed, "What are you doing,
naughty child?"

She screamed for help.
The neighbors came and
looked at the four-year-old,
a poker hanging from her body.
The laughter was uproarious,
and I plastered myself against
the wall,
not understanding what was
so funny.

I felt shame too.
Shame because I had bubbles,
in what do they call it —
my vagina.

The neighbors went away, while
I was left alone, humiliated.
Mamma was never told,
because what adult would
dare speak of such a thing?

The bubbles continued to spin
around and around.
One day, one of them
told me to call on a neighboring
boy of the same age.

We went to the forest,
and at the say-so of my bubbles,
I pulled down his pants.
He pulled down mine.
I put a blade of grass around
the place where he too had bubbles.

We laughed and laughed.
We both felt whole.
I'll never forget that whole feeling.
It was better than the cake, the
whipped cream, and the hot chocolate
in the cafe.

I'm left with my bubbles,
which get bigger as I get older.
I want to touch myself, but
do not dare.
I still remember being
plastered against the wall —
my face hanging down, tears
streaming from my eyes,
my bubbles, broken inside my
vagina,
from humiliation.

I squeezed my legs together
so the bubbles wouldn't escape.
They made my stomach sick,
because they got caught in my
body instead of fizzing through —
my vagina.

They gave me funny thoughts,
thoughts of having been a whore,
with many men —
men who wanted my vagina
and my bubbles.

I let the men have me, but
when it was over, they turned

their backs and left —
left me like Papa leaves and goes
to her, my mamma.

What's the use of having bubbles,
when they can't fizz and wiggle,
grow and explode,
renewing me, my energy, my thoughts,
joining with another with whom I
become whole?

What's the use when my parents
look at me and make me feel
ashamed?
They don't have bubbles.
They hardly touch one another.
Their bedroom door is always open.
Maybe that's why they yell and scream
at each other.

If I could exchange my bubbles with
someone else,
I would become whole.
Wouldn't the world become whole
if everyone's bubbles could fuse
lovingly with another being?
There is beauty in such a union.

Why don't they let me have my bubbles,
so the energy can wiggle and wobble,
fizz and explode,
to wholeness?

6

The Little Will

In response to those parental attempts to break my spirit, I invented at this time of my life what I call the "little will." I had conceived of it much earlier in my life, but now I put it into action as never before.

I had a great deal of energy. Consequently, my will was also energetic and powerful. I thought of it as like the propeller of an airplane, piercing its way through life, making a path for what I wanted to do. At first I thought of this will as "little," but the more energy I gave it, the larger it became, until it was like a giant shadow hovering over me. I fused with this will, never to separate from it. "No, no, no! I will not! Never! My way, not yours!" It encompassed my entire psyche until it felt like a multiplying machine, getting richer and more powerful with every breath I did not take, with every clench of the jaw and contraction of the back I did make.

It was clear to me that my will had to remain mute; if not, hell would have been a better place to live than my parents' home. My will and I went underground. There, in the subterranean passages of my psyche, we schemed and plotted about everything. When I felt frightened, my will would negate the fear by putting a film across my eyes so reality was blurred. In this way I was able to involve myself in many undertakings requiring courage.

For example, a teacher in school invited me to take dance lessons because she thought I might have talent in that art form. My mother objected. I did not bother to listen to her, but went into that secret cavern in my psyche where my will was housed, and together we decided I would take lessons anyway. I thought to myself, "The less I am like you, Mamma, the more I will respect myself."

I often forfeited lunch, using whatever allowance had been given me to pay for my dance lessons. Others made dance tunics for me and offered to launder them so Mamma would never find out. I stood straight and tall, despite my secrecy and scheming. I never realized to what degree this pattern of behavior would become my way of life.

My parents did not know of my outside activities. My will and I were experts at keeping our secrets hidden. When I was face-to-face with my mamma, I would smile and be gracious, always wary of her potential onslaught. To Papa I would give my Mona Lisa smile.

Often I would come home late from school because of a dance rehearsal. My will and I would have a "breezy" explanation to which Mamma would listen like a suspicious animal. When she asked, "Where were you, really?" my papa would rear into an upright position, shushing her into silence while he bolted from the table. He was as apprehensive about more warfare as I was. I thought he was protecting me. In time, I discovered he was mostly concerned about his own sanity.

My rationalizations for his behavior were: "Had he not been wounded in the war? Was not his nature fragile and sensitive? Was he not a soft-spoken, sweet-natured man?"

The reality was that he wanted to know nothing about her or me. He wanted only to read his newspaper and drink his "spritzer." From time to time, he would let me make one for him. "Too much wine," he would tease, as he looked delicately at me. My heart would burst. He knew I existed.

I wondered later in life if I had always given him too much wine so I might be the recipient of that sideways glance, a glance that sustained me for a long, long time. I took that glance into my room and bathed in it, particularly when Mamma was physically abusive to me.

My life consisted of secrets and lies, avoidance of Mamma's attacking hands, and the longed-for enigmatic glances from my papa. (I noticed that he would make certain her back was turned before he chanced this contact with his young daughter.) This was the home atmosphere and energy I became familiar with. Within the drama that bound us together, we continued existing in total isolation from one another. He would go to work in his shop, where he was considered a "saint." She was known to the neighbors as a beautiful, joyful woman who loved animals, who listened sympathetically to the woes of others, and who kept a spotless home. I was perceived as a talented, well-behaved child. Were they to look more closely they would have become aware of the fear in my eyes, my willful jaw, and my not-too-hidden need for love.

We lived in this atmosphere and grew older in it. She grew more furious. He drank more "spritzers" to soothe, so he said, the gnawing pains in his stomach. Approaching my teenage years, I became more depressed, feeling imprisoned in this house of bondage: a circular, twisted labyrinth where breathing was impossible. Breathing would have created too much feeling, consequently even more pain. It became apparent that they were killing one another and that I was the scapegoat for their misery. My aura reeked of their misery, their vindictiveness, their hatred. As a result I invited into my life more abuse from others, more abandonment, more aloneness.

The child in me was spinning webs and was eventually to be entangled in them. I could not cry out for fear of being heard; I could not break out of my turtle-like shell. It never occurred to me to attack that impenetrable tank, my mother. Had I dared to try, I could imagine the tank running over me with such precision and swiftness that not a solitary cell in my body would survive.

He, my delicate papa, was also fighting for his life. He stayed longer in his shop. He became more engrossed in himself and with his ailing right leg, which gave him more difficulty from year to year. The shrapnel wound began oozing gangrenous blood. It was poisonous blood; he had never stood on his leg like a strong man. Like a martyr, she ministered to his affliction. I looked upon his leg and wept silently. I was afraid I might lose him. Then what would become of me?

When he was in this physical state, he had the upper hand. He pleaded for silence in the house. She gave it to him, except when she thought I had transgressed in one way or another. She would then "tank" her way into our terrain and shoot us both down. When this occurred, he would leave the house with his hands across his ears. This was a bold act for him. It awakened her to another reality. I could imagine her thoughts at this point: "What will I do if he is serious? I have never worked here in America. How will I survive?" She stopped her tirades and called him back. Like a queen humbled, she made a spritzer for him as he reentered the door. He panted hard as he took his customary seat at the table. She ministered to his wounds once again. She gestured to me to leave the room.

When this happened, there was silence in the house. The Swiss clocks were ticking on the wall. The atmosphere had changed. For a few minutes I wanted to breathe and was able to. If only I could have captured this feeling and placed it in a bottle from which it could be dispensed, like drops of perfume. I felt my body relax, my jaw loosen, my shoulders soften. I felt the will between my shoulder blades let go so that, for once, I was bigger than it. That night, I slept soundly. I wished never to use my will again, but we both knew the quiet would not last. My will remained on vigilant guard, while I, Anneliese, slept with all my might.

I was eighteen years old. High school was over. I received honors and awards. Mamma told the neighbors, who praised her for having raised such a special daughter. She was proud, not for me, but for herself. She never congratulated me on my victories. I had also been given the opportunity to go to an elite college. My mother told my father about the honors I received. His response was to stand by the table in his usual way, reading his newspaper. He smiled his enigmatic smile without looking up. With a gesture of his right hand, he waved her away. He could not be disturbed, or excited, or feel, or think, or be anything but concerned with himself. His heart could not be stimulated; his wounded leg could not be strained.

I stood at the door, waiting, hopeful that some acknowledgment would come my way. It did not. The hope of getting their approval no longer stimulated me. However, I still insisted in my heart that my father must be very proud of me, for was he not my papa who loved me? This time even that hope felt limp.

I began to feel for the first time how alone I was. My only connection to them was that they fed, housed, and clothed me. I felt again, as I had earlier in my life, that I was in a rowboat, with no oars and no direction. I was out in the world like a dog with its tail between its legs, waiting for someone to acknowledge it.

"Stars, you know I exist, don't you?" I asked. "You blink and blink. Does that mean yes? Won't you come down and take me with you? What is beyond that dark, blue sky? Is it a world that is better than mine? It has to be, for I can still hear its music and smell the sweetness of the air. I can feel its peace. Deep inside me, I see the tall beings with their beautiful countenances, with bright, clear eyes. They say, 'Yes. You exist. You have that right. Be courageous and persevere. We are here for you. You have much to do on this earth.' " Thus I soothed my body and soul.

Even though I felt acknowledgment from the celestial beings, or the voices of my higher self, I went behind my eyes more than ever. It was difficult for me to perceive the outside world in any other way than as what I had known for eighteen years. I perceived women as tanks that would annihilate me swiftly should I assert myself. Men were like snowflakes, melting when they touched the earth.

Life was a willful, joyless state, to be endured. There were moments of satisfaction, however, in dance classes, rehearsals, and in school. But I had few friends. They rejected me in time because I did not have their understanding about life. I could not identify with their desires or their ways of living. I looked upon them with incredulity: that the females had male friendships; that they joked with one another; that they were sexually knowledgeable; that they had a social life which enabled them to stay out late; that they could banter with their parents and bring their friends to their homes. Life for them was a swinging door instead of a revolving one controlled by parents who made normal passage impossible.

I remembered at the age of eleven having the thought of either "letting go" into unreality or continuing to fight for my survival and sanity. I remembered thinking of the word "reincarnation," which I was unable to spell or understand. I recalled making the decision to continue with my struggles because I did not wish to return to another incarnation having to face the same painful experiences in yet one more life. As a result of this decision, I continued to fight to stay alive and to rally with my destiny.

How that idea entered my mind at that time baffles me. My conclusion was not dissimilar from the one recounted earlier when, as a newborn organism, following my father's brutal assault upon me, I had been faced with the choice of whether to remain on Earth or to leave my body and die.

That decision in preadolescence, ratifying the decision I made as an infant, was a turning point in my life. I can only surmise that in both instances my soul, or my intrinsic self, was speaking to me and guiding me, proving that my contact with that part of myself was vigilant and very much alive.

7

Late Adolescence

I started college but could not give my studies the same attention as in previous years. I was tired and depressed most of the time. I was exhausted from the constant battle with my mother, who was by now menopausal and more irrational and manic than ever. Her beauty had become marred by dermatitis; her mood swings were so intense that her fury with life was unabated. She blamed her husband, me, and America for her joyless state.

I longed to get out and secretly looked for other places to live, but found that I would not be able to cope with the outside world either emotionally or financially. I worked at a part-time job while going to college, hoping to dispel some of my mother's criticism about my wanting to educate myself further and my partial financial dependency on them. Nothing could satisfy her; the warfare continued on a daily basis.

Desperate for some reprieve from my mother's nagging and to become financially independent of them, I took a job as a dancer in a musical comedy theater. The performances were at night. Secrecy was of the utmost importance, for would not my parents consider theater people to be prostitutes and pimps? I pretended to leave for school early in the morning, walking the streets of New York until showtime, sitting in cafeterias, libraries, and friends' homes. I stopped college after two years, unable to concentrate, exhausted from the rigorous, senseless routine.

One morning I could not get out of bed. Weary and exhausted from the senseless routine of walking around the city, I revealed my dreaded secret. Luckily, fate was on my side, because my mother had discovered a salve which had cleared up her skin condition, restoring her to her usual narcissistic demeanor. She forced me to tell my papa of my dancing job, and he, bewildered by my unorthodox behavior, dismissed me from his presence. Mamma looked on happily.

I had met a young man a few years older than me. He thought I was beautiful, talented, everything a woman should be. I was overwhelmed by his ardent display of love. I did not respond to him with equal affection, but drank in every word and gesture of kindness he gave me, absorbing his thoughts and words like a plant that had never been watered. Drop by drop his magic words penetrated my being until a healing of the many psychic wounds took place. His name was Michael. I referred to him as "my whispering knight." He served me as a faceless, bodiless, amorphous Good Mother, one who poured love and good thoughts into a desperate psyche.

In my unreality about him, I did not observe that he was almost six feet tall. I did not see that he was ungainly in his body, constantly smiling, painting romantic pictures of me, his fairy princess, whom he was rescuing from my monstrous parents. I did not understand that he bathed in my innocence, my gullibility, my neediness. I did not comprehend that he was unconsciously luring me into his den of unreality. I was unaware, until, one day, he jolted me out of my "being nurtured" state by his suggestion that I leave my parents' home to live with him.

I shook my head wildly as I pictured the scene that would take place with my parents should I propose such a thing to them. I pushed him away from me. He groped for me, desperately reassuring me that he had patience and that he would wait forever if necessary.

It slowly dawned on me that he had withdrawn his request, that I could once again sink into the security of his presence, a presence without demands, without obligations: the presence of an eternal Mother. I sensed, however, that the matter was only temporarily postponed. I knew that soon I would have to face my parents' inquisition about Michael, that there would be a severe trial, if not for the both of us, then certainly for me.

Throughout our relationship I had monitored our caresses carefully, fearful that any intimate transgressions might be detected by my sleuthlike mother. We would stand on the corner of my street, embracing each other, while I, at the same time, peeked out of the corner of my eye for signs of my parents' heads suspended from our fifth-floor tenement window. If I saw them, I flew from Michael's embrace like Batman, whizzing through the air. When I arrived at the top of the stairs of our apartment building, I was yanked through the door by their four hands and plunked into the nearest seat, which felt like an electric chair. I was interrogated. I answered all their questions.

Papa finally announced that this would be the last time, the very last time. I did not understand what he meant. Did he mean this was the last time I would be subjected to their irrationality: the last time I would remain chained in their house of bondage? In time, however, the mysterious statement became clear by itself.

I successfully auditioned the following day for an overseas theatrical event that took me to Germany and France. It was the time of the Second World War. I had been hired for a musical comedy troupe that was scheduled to play to the soldiers of the American army. We rehearsed for four weeks, after which we found ourselves in a convoy of ships headed for Le Havre.

The departure of the convoy was a military secret. The secrecy of the trip enabled me to avoid personal farewells on the dock, releasing me from false sentiments about separation from my parents as well as from Michael. Michael and I promised to correspond with one another, but I gave little thought to this promise other than its being a sense of connection to the self he had awakened in me since our first meeting. My parents had little to say about my departure, other than its being opportune for gaining information of any survivors who were kin. I realized that their interest in my trip had little to do with my proudly-earned role in the show; as usual, my accomplishments were incidental.

The engagement with the show whisked me away, away from one hell to, perhaps, a hell of another kind — that of wartime. The future was unknown as I left New York harbor. I did feel, however, that I had an opportunity for freedom.

Halfway across the Atlantic Ocean, the performers and the soldiers on the ships were informed that the war in Europe had ended. We were overjoyed and relieved; external danger was over. I now had only myself to deal with. I was twenty-four years old and for the first time in my young life, the external terror by which I had always been surrounded would be absent. The psychic chains that had compressed my existence fell away. I stretched my liberated body and spirit and proceeded to go wild.

8

Reaching Toward the Male

I found myself liberated as the Allies had been liberated. I was like a crazed animal that had been caged forever. At first I remained closeted in my "not I" state, hiding in its hole until I slowly and cautiously opened the door to the outside world. I reveled in the warmth of the air in my nostrils and sensed the energy of the men of the Army, who had also been caged for the last four years or more, who had lived in a state of fear and terror. We smelled each other's longing to be touched, accepted, desired. These awarenesses in me became ignited by my newly-found freedom. Its energy rushed to the perimeters of my body until I glowed, sparkled, and shone.

In Germany, the show was a success. The soldiers hailed us as though we were the conquerors, not they. After each performance, they hooted, howled, screamed, threw their hats into the air, and asked for encores. They were starved for connections to their homeland in song, in dance, in the American language, in the cast of women and men who looked familiar to them. We were wooed, we were adored, we were their salvation until the machinery of war could be reversed and they could return to America.

I, too, hooted, howled, and screamed with pleasure as each day unfolded for me. Each night became a gala event for the players, with invitations to parties in castles, in elegant homes that had been captured by the Allies, or to dinner parties with the enlisted men in their dining rooms.

I became sexually involved with an officer, one of high rank, who had a wife back home. That he was a married man did not deter me. I did not care. It made the adventure more enticing. "Perhaps he will replace her with me," was my thought, when I had any thought at all. I was living actively, moving from impulse to impulse. "Perhaps I will win the man, despite the other woman," was another fleeting thought I had, as our liaison became an established fact. At the same time, almost every man became a potential target for my seductive attack. My senses had gone berserk. I was in the momentum of experiencing myself for the first time in many years. Nothing could stop me.

Since the war had ended only a few weeks before, curfews were still in effect. All lights were to be extinguished by a certain time and we were to be in our quarters. I defied these rules, as did my lover, who waited for me at the foot of my bedroom balcony. But there was no long-winded balcony scene as in *Romeo and Juliet*. Instead, he grabbed my hands while I scrambled down a tree, adjacent to my room. We twittered with excitement as we stole away to a place he had arranged for our rendez-vous. My escape was reminiscent of those from my not-too-long ago curfew. This time, however, I was the commander of my action. There were no heads popping out of windows, ready to destroy me, no electric chair that awaited me while I was being interrogated and sentenced. The danger now was one I exulted in defying, for I knew that the anticipated experience would be one of pleasure, loving, and being understood.

I sensed within myself an overwhelming lust for a man, an insatiable desire to pull him into me, to devour him and make him mine. This lust felt like part of a primitive rite that lay dormant in the subterranean, archaic layers of my psyche. My lover, too, was smitten and overwhelmed. He would mutter that he was a married man and that I should not forget. However, the sound of the words and their meaning became unimportant as he fell limp and satisfied from the consummated act so important to both of us.

In our more gentle, quiet moments, I found him to be a sweet, warm, kind man, one of eight siblings. He was in great need of love and attention. I gave those to him and I received those from him. We were like two starved animals in a nest that had been forsaken by the parents. He needed the security of a woman and marriage. He had intimated that his wife was not fertile. This encouraged me to attempt to win him over from the other woman. I glowed inwardly, taking possession of him all the more.

I was enthralled with the secrecy of my relationship with my officer. I was enthralled with our rendezvous and the inventiveness needed by both of us to steal from my room and to return to it in the early morning. We plotted endlessly how to avoid detection. My psyche was attuned to the excitement; I had had proper training from my environment in matters of stealth, deceit, and secrecy. We had to be particularly careful about our intimacy because of his status in the Army. When we attended parties sponsored by his elite group of officers, in castles, mansions, or the like, we would eye one another over our champagne glasses while conversing with others. Our looks would convey the memory of the sweetness of the night before, as well as that of the moment before the party, when we had embraced in some dark corner.

We would remember how much we had wanted each other. He would excuse himself from the other officers and stumble to my group, introducing himself to them and to me, as though for the first time. Our eyes would meet and melt into one another. The others would be taken aback but never realize our ruse. They would quietly excuse themselves, leaving us to ourselves, while they refilled their glasses with champagne. The two of us would remain invisibly entwined and plan our next rendezvous. I sensed I had him in my power but that he would eventually bore me. My arrogance was boundless.

On this particular night, some of the singers of our theatrical troupe were called upon to perform. This was always a delightful event. The nostalgic songs took each participant back to the warmth and security of the environment they had left behind.

It was at this point that old memories, old unwanted realities entered my mind. I remembered that I was homeless. I remembered the words of my papa about its being "the last time, the very last time." I recalled the reality of my whispering knight, with whom I was sporadically in contact through the mail. The memory of Michael felt like a life raft to me, but it made me joyless. I recalled our first meeting. His face seemed always to be disposed to an acne condition, though, in fact, this condition did not exist. Was I intuiting an aspect of his inner being which repulsed me and kept me distant from him? Or was the hateful nature of my mother already in operation in my "not I" state? He had become my voices, good voices that fed my psyche while we were together. I felt dependent on him, but I knew the excitement I was now feeling with the officer was absent.

I looked around me to see my married lover lost in nostalgia. I could sense his thoughts about his wife. As the songs finished and as each person emerged from his or her reverie, they automatically headed to the bar for more champagne. My lover did also. I felt so alone. Again I had been left for the other woman. It was an unbearable feeling. I left the party without an explanation to anyone. I went to my bedroom and slept fretfully, racked with pain. It was the old pain of aloneness, lovelessness, and desertion. It pervaded me totally. My will was not available. It had had too much to drink.

I awakened the next morning with a steel jaw, a renewed iron will, my face set in a masklike vise, determined never to be hurt again. No one, nothing, would ever penetrate this demeanor of mine. These were my thoughts as I sat alone at the breakfast table. With every sip of coffee that entered my mouth, I became more determined that this would be my state for eternity. I made myself an oath that I would never again endure another night like the one that had just passed. This oath was in the process of becoming law when one of the members of the cast thrust a note into my hand.

The note was from my lover. He pleaded with me to meet him under our trysting tree at an appointed time. I was gleeful. "He needs me more than I need him," was my thought. I felt intense relief. The world became suddenly more radiant. I felt my willful jaw relax. My agonized brain became less knotted. I began to savor the hot brew which I was sipping while, at the same time, a delighted smile appeared on my face. I finished my breakfast and, with a newly-found desire to live, walked to meet him at our trysting tree.

He was waiting, pacing anxiously. I relished this excitement. I ran into his arms without caution. He kissed my face, kissing away the tears. We held each other in the daylight, knowing our secret was exposed. He kept asking why I had left. Did I not know of his feelings toward me? I was dizzied by the range of emotions. He scooped me into his arms and we ran to our secret quarters. We talked and loved and loved and talked for many hours. We were two beings who needed the assurance from each other that we were wanted. The old wounds of not being wanted were healed for the moment; we bathed in our acceptance of each other; our needs were insatiable.

I knew within myself that he would never leave his wife. I also intuited that I would not wish him to, for I felt he was not strong enough to handle me in my "not I" state. I dimly realized that within me there was a desire to hurt him, perhaps even to mutilate him. But these intuitive sparks of awareness represented the extent to which my unclear conscious-ness revealed itself. I could not yet believe that the other extreme of being victimized by men was to be the victimizer — nor that my psyche was capable of that.

I wondered why we had been brought together. I had learned from him how tender and loving a man could be. I was also aware that I eventually would malign as weak and ineffectual any man who genuinely cared for me; I was more comfortable with a man's confused feelings toward me than with the sensation of being wanted unreservedly. My officer did not know, nor did I, if we would ever see one another again. I doubted it but wondered what would be our destiny.

Since the end of the tour was approaching, I withdrew into my willful state and prepared for our separation. I was shocked at how little I felt when we parted.

He wished for us to remain in contact. He had asked to have a child with me, which he and his wife could adopt. It was at that precise moment that my detestation of men had escalated. "He wants a part of me," I thought, "but he will not give himself to me fully." It was a painful realization, too reminiscent of my life at home with my papa. I had become accustomed to being betrayed by men. Unbeknown to me, I expected little else than betrayal, mixed with sporadic moments of pleasure and acceptance. He was not aware of the exact moment he had shattered my good feelings toward him, but when he looked into my face, he saw eyes filled with hatred.

I was anxious to get away from him, to leave him well behind as a memory that had brought joy, pleasure, excitement, and romance, along with a deep sense that I would never be able to have those things again. I left him behind physically as I boarded a vessel which brought me and the company members back to America. Emotionally, his image disappeared as soon as I made other contacts on board the ship filled with returning American soldiers.

I was vaguely aware of the cruelty in my nature, aware that it was possible for me to disconnect from another with a flick of the eye. I became aware how capable I was of creating an unbridgeable chasm between me and others, all the while feeling like the victim who was mercilessly brutalized.

In retrospect I understand how important it was for me at that time to remain in my "not I" state. It was vastly more comfortable to blame him for not being available, keeping me trapped in my mother's tank-like nature, than to face the welter of my real feelings.

9

A Shadow Marriage

Fear, fear,
push away reality.
Ship, ship,
never come to shore.
Ride the seas,
until eternity
claims my body and spirit.

There, there,
upon the shore,
stands the whispering knight,
smiling, planning, droning, wanting
to possess his fairy princess again.

No other place to go,
except into his arms.
They feel so wrong,
so undefined, so insubstantial;
I have no other choice.

Life, life,
you frighten me.
He'll be my life raft.
Courage, courage,
where are you hiding?
Unavailable,
entrenched in fear.

Stay, stay,
within his grasp.
Shut out his droning.
"You are, you are,"
he chatters on,
"my princess unsurpassed."

Up in that tower,
where we reside,
sheltered, sheltered,
far from the world.
Oh God, life is boring.

The other world is Papa and Mamma,
a world that has to be faced.
I returned to America.
They have to be seen.
I brought mementoes
from kin.

I shared with Papa and Mamma
my experiences,
with their parents, relatives, and friends.
They listened and cried.
They looked at me gratefully.
But when the last picture

had been seen,
Papa returned to his newspaper
and read,
as though I were not present.

To get his attention,
Mamma poked his ribs with her elbow.
"Your daughter must be pregnant,"
said she smugly.
"Where is she staying?
With what man does she sleep?
She is pregnant!
I know. I can smell it."

I enter the bathroom,
vomiting at her behavior,
vomiting at the thought of pregnancy.
When I return, she is hysterical,
her elbow becoming more active.
Papa responds at last.
He looks at me in disgust.

"She's pregnant. She must be.
Look how she vomits.
She's rounder and fuller.
Those are the signs.
We'll not take care of you,
nor his child.
Let him, whoever he is,
be responsible."

"Get married," they both scream,
"or never come to this house again.
You'll not make a laughingstock of us.

You made your bed,
now lie in it.
That's the right way!
We had to."

I flee from their household,
debased and humiliated,
wondering what to do next.
"Shall I marry the whispering knight,
as they demanded?
But he is not my beloved,
not the right mate."

He will come, he will come,
but not until I'm stronger.
In the meantime, I'll rest in
the knight's false embrace.
I need more courage, more self.
In time, the rewards will
manifest.

To marry, to marry.
If not,
Papa will disown me.
This thought drowns me in pain.
Disowned by my Papa,
my other life raft?
His banishment would destroy me.

What to do?
What to do?
How can I forge a marriage certificate?
A certificate will appease him,
allay his fears of my becoming

a whore,
never wed, shunned by society,
his daughter —
a whore.
Was he responsible?

I'll go to a stationer.
I'll forge all names,
the clerk's, the judge's,
the knight's, and mine.
Papa will never know;
he is too frightened
to face reality clearly.

I go to his shop.
He looks at me tenderly.
He examines the forgery.
He asks tentatively, apologetically,
"Should it not have a seal?"
"No, Papa," I answer quickly.

He returns it to me,
not daring to ask further.
He gives me a wedding band,
an engagement ring as well.
"It's beautiful," I say,
"so many diamonds."

He beams —
he shows me affection.
It is clear Mamma is not around.

"He loves me.
He truly loves me," —

the litany begins.
It continues when I leave him,
a mantra my mind has devised.
The words were hollow,
but they assuaged my terror of aloneness.

I sat in a park for many hours, thinking:
"I am what thieves, liars, murderers,
prostitutes are made of.
Oh, God, why did you
bring the ship to shore?
Why do you make beings
spineless and terrified?
Take them back and redo them!"

I walked like a ghost
to our citadel.
My knight was waiting for me,
wondering where I had been.
"With this one, with that one,"
I twittered on aimlessly.
"Did you know so-and-so
got into a show?"

"My fairy princess," he whispered,
"I adore you."
"You wouldn't adore me," I said to myself,
"if you knew who I really am and
what I am capable of.
But, as a matter of fact, I would cast you
aside if I had the courage
I need."

He wanted to love me,
to consummate his passion.
"It's painful," I said to him.
I'd become skillful in warding him off,
but I did not understand my lack of
attraction. I did not realize our
incompatible chemistry left me
without desire.

"My chaste, pure angel," he responded.
"My princess!"
"Oh, God," I thought, "what a farce.
What a joke — his chaste, pure
princess! After my escapades with the
officer — whom I cruelly left behind,
whose wife I betrayed!

"Who am I, God? Who am I, really?
I can't continue this charade.
But I'm filled with the terror of being
alone, of being in the world,
which reminds me of my parents.
I can't continue.
I'd rather die."

"Come to bed, fairy princess,"
he whispered in the background.
"I'll come to bed, but don't touch me.
I'm fragile like a butterfly — "
        "Like Papa,"
I thought to myself.
"But we're both hidden monsters inside.

"A monster like me, like him."
These were my insistent thoughts.
"Like you," answered the echoing voice.
But this was too much for my "not I"
state to absorb.
"I'm a chaste, pure, fairy princess,"
I implored.

"Come to bed, come to bed,"
he whispered again.
"I'm coming. I'm coming," I told him
willingly.
"Drown out, drown out
those unwanted voices.
Drone on, drone on,
my enchanted prince."

"You are pure, chaste, so beautiful,
so talented," he whispered.
His voiced faded away as he gave
a startling snore, whispering,
"My fairy princess, whom I will
love forever."

I crawled around his adulating words
until sleep overcame me.
In the morning, I felt fear, disgust,
terror of reality.
"When will this end?" I asked those
in the heavens.
"When you face who you are,"
the voices echoed.

I can't—not yet.
My "not I" state

serves this terror well.
I cling to you, terror,
a while longer.
And with it, the knight and
our joyless, deadly existence.

"I'm a pure, chaste, beautiful
monster —
a fairy princess —
a wicked witch.

"Oh God, who am I really?
Really?"

Really?! Really?!
"You are —
You are not!"
was that unwanted response.
"Why can't I leave him?"

We continued like this
for another year.
We argued and bickered constantly.
We could not connect,
we were made of different substances.
Our relationship remained static.

He, too, was bored,
but would not acknowledge it.
Seeing one another
became tedious.

One day, I told him,
"We must separate;

we are stifling each other."
The dreaded word had been articulated.
He agreed.
He knew it would be useless
to hang on to a relationship
that made him feel
unwanted and used,
like a mother's teats.

We set a date for the fateful day.
He droned on endlessly
about the wicked world.
I promised I would call him
if tragedy befell me.
Was he not my knight who
understood the chaste, beautiful
princess whom he feared
could be destroyed by the ugly world?

I shut out his droning,
immersed in my own terror.
He left the apartment.
I was alone.
Did I miss him?
Did I long for him?
I could not say for certain.
He was a phantom in my psyche,
an attachment which had given
me solace.

It was over, it was over.
I opened myself to living.
At times, I experienced joy.
In a short while I met Sean,

the antithesis of Michael.
Another part of me became realized.

Who am I, God?
Who am I, really?
The mystery unfolds.
The path to my Self continues.

10

The Wild Irish Lover

No sooner had my whispering knight vacated our apartment than I was discovered by Sean at a party. He was a college literature professor, seven years older than I, who looked into my eyes with the intent of devouring me. His gaze was direct and honest, his enchanting brogue as thick as Irish ale. It was summertime; Sean spent his vacation from college at the beach as a lifeguard.

He lived in his body like an animal finely tuned not only to itself but to nature. He was most happy in the ocean, frolicking with the waves, sensing their movement, releasing his being to the ferocity and roar of the water. I would watch his body tumbling from one wave to the other. I sensed he was lost to the voices of the water as he fused with the water's essence.

He awakened me sexually so my body ached for his presence. I was relieved to find that my sexuality was not amiss, as it had been with Michael, but heightened to such an extent that I desired him constantly. He was loving, kind, and unpredictable. I never knew when he would make an appearance.

I found his unpredictability exciting; it was a contrast to the monotony of my previous relationship. I would not hear from him or see him for many days, to be surprised by his appearance in the waiting room of my dance classes or at the doorstep of my apartment. We would rush home, wordless, until privacy was available. Our bodies were magnetized; our groping arms and hands would touch, caress, enfold each other's body like two Sivas bringing the ecstasy of the heavens onto the earth.

We were connected in this amazing way, feeling the stars explode with a burst of applause and gratitude for the other's existence. He knew every nuance of my nature and was not afraid of it. Instead, he responded to it from his intuitive self, asserting his maleness all the more when any irascible qualities of my "not I" state emerged.

Michael would promptly have gone into his drone at any indication of irascibility. I would have fallen into despair and the energy between us would have died. It was a new experience to be intuited by someone, accepted and cajoled into a more vibrant, balanced state. I adjusted to his erratic entrances and exits in my life and, for a while, was excited by this new relationship.

From time to time I would be in contact with Michael. We would dine together, talk familiarly about the things we had shared. I felt at ease with this connection, as though I were speaking with an old friend. We parted, feeling that perhaps at some future time we might wish to resume our relationship. I wished that sexually it could be as I found it with Sean. The energy between us was not of that nature, however. Once, after a long evening together, saddened by this realization, I left Michael's apartment. It was early morning as I walked home, musing and wondering what my destiny was with that man or any man.

As I approached my apartment, I was surprised and fearful to see the windows brightly lit. When I opened the door, Sean was asleep on the bed. He had pried open a window to gain access to the apartment. I was furious. It was the first time I felt invaded by his spontaneous impulses.

As I prepared myself for bed, he awakened. Since direct expression of feelings was still difficult for me, I hid my anger and brushed by him without words. He got hold of my arm, asking me where I had been. This kind of interrogation was reminiscent of my life with my parents. I became paralyzed with fear but told him the truth.

He muttered that it would not surprise him if I returned to Michael. The idea registered in my brain. I became confused by what I really wanted. I must have looked bewildered. He, like a stalking animal sensing the weakness in its prey, drew me to him passionately. He could not drink me into himself strongly enough. It was as though he were branding me for life, to make me his forever. His phallic nature could not be satisfied.

Finally, when his instincts told him I was again his, he left. I lay on the bed emptied of self. "If only Michael's intellect could be blended with Sean's primitive instincts," I thought, "perhaps I would have a whole man."

It never occurred to me that the lack of wholeness was within me. I realized much later through the therapeutic process that I attracted these men to me for that reason. My experiences with them would remain mere interesting shifts in life's richness unless I was willing to examine my lack of wholeness. I did not do so until later.

In the meantime, Sean came and went as he pleased. Dates were never kept as they should have been. It was not a question of other women; he needed time to recoup his male energy so he could encompass my female energy.

Sean detested his father and adored his mother. His mother, afraid of her husband's brutality, had often betrayed her children in order to keep his father supporting the family. Sean became confused: his rageful feelings toward his father were clear, while his feelings toward his mother and all women were muddled.

I did not understand then that his absences between our meetings were needed to reorganize his libido so that he could conquer me. He needed to disengage himself from his confusion toward his mother in order to bring his sexual strength to me. Since there was an uncanny synchronicity between us, it was not difficult for him to conquer and for me to be conquered. It was in the silence, however, after our wild, bodily engulfing of each other, that I felt bored once again.

I could not resist those exquisite sexual experiences with him, though. Again and again, I surrendered to him, becoming a shooting star, falling from the heavens to land on the earth, back in my body. He, too, could not resist the energy between us.

I became aware during our sleep of the relentless, persistent fury within him. It made me want to leave his embrace while he was sleeping. In the morning, we noticed that the position of my body indicated my wish to leap out of his arms, like a diver, emerging from the bottom of the ocean, straining for a desperate gasp of air.

Sean seldom turned inward for emotional information about himself, despite the fact that he was extremely perceptive about me. He raved and ranted about the world's injustices, which made me mute and bored. I would secretly wish for him to leave after our lovemaking.

I said nothing but, more and more, thought of rejoining my whispering knight.

11

Three Men and a Ship

Three men and a ship —
what is my story?
I went to Europe again.
Three years had passed
since I saw my grandparents,
my relatives, my friends.

I'm on a great liner,
headed for Le Havre.
My parents saw me off.
They brought gifts,
for me and their kin.

My knight came too,
in the role of a dutiful husband.
Although we had been separated
for almost a year,
neither parent detected our secret.
Michael played the role superbly.

He held my hand
at the appropriate times.
He gave me affectionate hugs.
These gestures tantalized my mother
and embarrassed my father.
We looked like an ideal couple.

I had remembered to wear my
wedding ring.
Mamma noticed the many diamonds.
She counted the number,
then confronted Papa:
"She's got more diamonds than I have."

Poor Papa became distraught.
He sensed there would be another upheaval.
I rescued him,
took him on the deck.
He said little,
but I knew he was grateful.

We were alone, a rare event.
He tried to ask questions.
He could not express his feelings.
I felt compassion for his awkwardness,
relieved by
Michael's and Mamma's appearance.

They showed up,
looking exceedingly uncomfortable.
They needed to be rescued.
I did what I could
to change the situation,
but I felt I needed to move mountains.

I am stuck in this stupid mess:
a husband who is not my husband,
a papa, terrified,
my mamma, who wishes me dead.

"Why did I choose
these characters for my life's drama?"
I did not understand until later.
In the meantime, my life rafts,
Michael and Papa,
served to make me feel
I was wanted.

The ship's whistle blew —
twelve o'clock,
time to depart.
They opened a champagne bottle.
All drank with gusto,
murmuring, "Bon voyage."

The three went down the gangplank
and stood by the vessel.
They waved and pantomimed
their feelings.
I was engaged in this drama
when, from the distance,
came shouts of,
"Anneliese! Anneliese!"

It was Sean,
unpredictable as usual,
waving a handbag in the air.

It was his present for my departure.
He screamed loud; all could hear him:
"Write to me. I'll answer."

The three on the dock
observed the spectacle.
They were in shock.
They turned to him and then
in my direction
until, exasperated, they
stood like robots,
wondering what
that man had to do with me.

Sean jumped up and down:
"Anneliese!
The traffic held me up!"
I jumped up and down:
"You're full of blarney!
You always have
an excuse for being late."

But our energies were alive,
not like it was with the others.
"Sean loves me," was my thought.
I shouted back to him:
"I'll write!"
It was then that my parents
bolted from the dock.

My whispering knight
stood paralyzed,
feeling he had been used again.
He was saddened —

Was I not his fairy princess,
his chaste maiden for eternity?

He left the dock,
his shoulders hunched,
while Sean kept bobbing
up and down.
I have some love, even
though it's distorted.
The ship sailed from the dock.

Three men
were interested in Anneliese.
They filled my empty insides with
warmth.
It did not matter the nature
of their interest:
I was wanted, I was loved,
I was not alone.

Sean's unpredictable telephoning
followed me throughout my journey.
We never connected.
His attempts fanned my illusions:
He wants me.
I'm loved.
I'm not alone.
I can be.

The truth of the matter
was not important.

"Child of God,
pathetic child.

One of many illusions.
Your house of cards will tumble down,
unless you face reality." *

"Not I. Not yet,"
was all I could muster.
"Tomorrow —
may it never come.
I'll stay behind my eyes,
until I'm forced —
to see,
to understand,
to feel pain,
to rectify.

"Life! Life!
don't vanquish me.
Treat me kindly."
"I'll treat you
as you treat me,"
was its answer —
answer.

Three men,
who are you?
Three men, unreal,
whom I could not see.

---

* *This bold-italic type designates another voice in my awareness, an enlightened voice, that of the Higher Self.*

They were
all
as blind
as
me.

12

Two Goodbyes

Upon my return from Europe, I felt obligated to call my parents. To my dismay I discovered that my papa had been hospitalized with bleeding stomach ulcers.

I spent the night in anguish. My papa was ill; he could no longer stomach my mother's poisonous negativity; he had not been able to energize his legs sufficiently to stand on them like a whole man. Had I not left our prison, mine as well as his, he would have been spared her wrath; he might not be ill. I was to blame for leaving him alone with her. "Oh God," I thought, "let him come out of this alive. I promise I will take care of him. I will make spritzers for him exactly the way he wants. I will help him in his work and dance only part-time."

I recalled that before my trip to Europe, he had asked me to help him sell his jewelry. He was too shy to assert himself in the world; consequently his business was failing. I dozed and awakened and thrashed about throughout the night, waiting impatiently for daylight, to visit him in the hospital.

I sat like a statue in the waiting room of the hospital. My defenses and my will were like generals in action. My body was breathless. I looked straight ahead of me, not blinking, not feeling the panic inside my abdomen, not tuning into my thumping heart. I was frozen, wishing for time to stand still.

65

I commanded from deep within my terrified state that nothing move, no one make a sound, that all life become immobilized, until the operation was over and my papa was out of danger. I had seen him briefly while they were preparing him for it. He seemed happy to see me and told me he realized how much he valued life and would never be flippant with it again.

"Where is Mamma?" I asked. He told me she had gone home to have some soup. She had left a message that I should join her.

"She went home to have some soup?" was my incredulous, silent response. I was aghast at her conspicuous lack of feeling for this man. I sat, instead, in the waiting room for hours, motionless. Nurses, attendants, doctors passing by became concerned about me. Time was frozen. Even though I was far away from him, it was as though I was glued to my papa, like his etheric body, giving him strength and energy to survive. I sat like a wall, I looked like a wall in the waiting room. No one dared approach me; I looked forbidding.

At the same time I was deeply engrossed by my papa's condition, I also sensed the drama I was creating. I had erected a wall behind which were buried a myriad of complicated feelings that I could not release in a normal expressive manner. They were of love, longing, hate, distrust; of disappointment, of frustration. There was also murderous rage. All coexisted at once. When one of the feelings needed an outlet, others would compete so ferociously that my innards felt like a football scrimmage. On the outside, however, I looked like a wall—a dramatic wall.

My statuesque frozenness aroused sympathy in my father's surgeon. He presented himself to me after the surgery, announcing that my papa was in the recovery room. He was adamant that I go home to rest, promising I would be notified of his condition. My "no" was emphatic. When he saw my obstinacy, he suggested I go home with him, to his family, where news of my father's progress would be immediately available. I shook my queenly head and stayed, responding to some intuitive presentiment within me.

Shortly after the surgeon's departure, a nurse called me into my papa's room. He was breathing with the help of oxygen. I lifted the oxygen cover and, for the first time in my life, told him from a tiny crack within my wall that I loved him. It felt like a frog's croak as I released those unfamiliar words. He must have heard me from within his wall, in which he too was solidly encased. He shushed me, then waved me away. Weakly, he said, "Go, get your mother." Mamma was not to be gotten, however. She was at home feeding her stomach. I told him so.

What followed was the miracle of my life. He might have finally understood her relationship to him, he might have finally become clearer about her relationship to me, or he might have understood nothing at all. He turned slightly toward me, however, and said, "She was not good to you, but — she did not mean it." After this unexpected, never-to-be-forgotten confession, the attending nurse asked me to leave.

I staggered out of the room repeating again and again, "He knew, Papa knew; he told me that he knew." I felt I was not crazy, that I had not been fabricating a case against her.

Since I was still in a "not I" state, his declaration made my papa more of a hero than ever. I had had an ally. It never occurred to me until many years later to ask: "Then why didn't you help me? Where were you? Why did you let me take the brunt of her fury? Where were you?"

He died shortly after our meeting. My mother had missed his exit from this world, but that was fitting, since they had missed each other throughout their lives. I did not cry. I did not mourn. I maintained my statuesque, frozen attitude about my papa and continued my convoluted pattern of behavior with men. I was too bottled up with years of unconscious, accumulated negativity toward him to have any other perceptions of him, and consequently of any man.

She, however, raved and ranted when I told her of his demise. Her immediate reaction was: "How could he do this to me?" The underlying tone of her mourning was: "What will become of me?"

I noticed that her gaze became fixed in my direction. I also noticed that she had placed me in his bed, next to hers, the night of his death. I had been too weary to be conscious of the meaning of her gesture. But thereafter, I repulsed every effort she made toward me. I relinquished the money he left me in his will, so she would not depend upon me.

I did not love her. I could not love her. I would not love her. I knew that contact with her would mean death for me. I closed the gates, locked them, and threw away the key. I did not care what the neighbors thought, nor her friends, nor the relatives. Thereafter, until her death eight years later, my visits to her were infrequent. I stood my ground about my distancing.

> I cry for Anneliese,
> whose child I am,
> whose eyes could not see,
> whose ears could not hear,
> whose voice could not speak,
> whose breath could not breathe,
> whose brows were contracted
> into a perpetual frown
> that said to the world:
>
> "I don't understand.
> Why am I here,
> if you do not care?
> To make me your victim,
> as you were for your parents?
> Why would you not tune
> into me, your child?
> Why could you not give me
> the love that I needed?"
>
> You could not.
> You would not.
>
> It might have been different,
> had you only asked,

"How can we cherish this little babe,
who is the flesh of our flesh,
free from our archaic hate?

"We cannot.
We will not.
Our parents did the same.
They hated their offspring,
as we do you now.

"We cannot.
We will not.
It must be this way.

"Honor your parents,
is what we say.
We will not do differently.
We would not if we could.
Vengeance pervades us:
It is for your own good."

It might have been different,
I say once again,
had you only asked:

"How do we cherish
this wondrous creation,
who would show us the way
to truer selves,
a revelation?"

You would have discovered
three happy beings,

who made life a gift,
ending this disease.

I cry for Anneliese,
whose child I am.
It was her fate
that to you she was born.

PART TWO

The "I"

*Man is a born child, his power is the
power of growth.*

*Man's history is waiting in patience
for the triumph of the insulted man.*

— Tagore

13

Becoming the "I"

In its ideal state, the "I" is erect,
strong, assertive, good, and concerned.
It has fear, doubt, unhappiness.
All are handled with a heart
that is open and free to express
its innermost pains.

It cries, it screams, it is angry, it has joy.
It loves delicately, it loves fiercely,
it hates.
It makes mistakes, it cheats, it lies.
It is lazy, it is ambitious,
it is honest.

It gives, it is given to.
When it is not given to,
it becomes resentful or understands.
It is like a weathervane turning swiftly
in the breeze, reacting, moving,
addressing.

It loves, it marries and has offspring.
It loves, but does not marry and it
lives alone.
It is the self that springs
from a healthier id.
It lives in the world and relates.
It goes hither and yon to see
how others live.
It connects, it appreciates, it denies.
It wants wealth, success, and renown.
It obtains them through integrity or deceit.

It has respect for this life.
It feels life in every pore:
How the sun's energy fuses with its body,
the water cleanses its skin,
the air makes the atmosphere fresher,
the earth provides for its nourishment,
the ether gives it its blessing.

All elements provide "I" with the
richness of being,
connecting to it with pleasure.
"I" knows what a valorous effort
it has taken to master itself in
the world.

There is pain in this "I."
There is longing
to fulfill itself further,
to go beyond.
It wills itself to become grateful,
to dance to life's rhythms,
aware that the earth is its ground.

"I" is proud to be handling Earth's
experiences,
masterful of its existence.
That is preferable to living in a "not I" state,
for "I" knows that living brings consciousness
and strength.

The "I" becomes a force in the psyche,
amassing and adding to
experiences that are needed
to make the being fuller.

14

The Seven-Year Itch

God,
You made the world
in seven days —
a magic number.

Was it Your intent
to dangle Sean before me
every seven years,
seven years,
every seven, seven years?

Jung calls such meetings
synchronous.
I call them mysterious,
uncanny,
and painful.

I cannot dispel
the image of Sean's waving arm
on the dock,

before the vessel
to Europe departed.

The next time his arm was visible
was in the giant waves
on a faraway beach,
a beach I was drawn to
in search of him.

Uncanny!
Without question!
The beach extended for six miles.
Why should I be drawn to one spot,
look into the distance,
and discover
his arm waving,
"Hi!"

He swam to shore;
he greeted me warmly.
We sat and talked
as though time were nonexistent.

"I'm married, you know,"
said Sean, after a few moments.
"Rebound—didn't like being
the other man on the dock."

I held my breath.
How familiar!
Sean was now unavailable.
I pushed the fact aside,

convinced I could win him over.
He said he'd call.
He did —
seven years later.

Was I upset?
Devastated!
I waited for the phone
to ring,
to hear that familiar
Irish brogue and laughter,
but the call never came.

We met again,
seven, seven years later.

Addicted to the ocean,
I sat by its edge,
in a lonely place.

Did you direct me there,
God?
I wanted to heal my
heart and soul.

I heard my name,
uttered in a melodious
Irish lilt.
When I looked up,
I saw Sean beside me.
He said:
"Wait.
I want to wipe the city's
grime off my body."

He plunged into the water.
When he reappeared,
he sat beside me.
Time was insignificant.
The eternity between us
reigned.

He told me forcefully,
"I'm divorced.
She has our child.
I should have waited
and married you.
We might have killed one
another," he continued, laughing,
"but it would have been
an adventure."

"It's my mistake.
There will be others."
He cried.
I held him tenderly.
He promised to call me
the following day.
I waited with longing
as well as trepidation.
The call never came.

I saw him again.
When?
Seven, upon seven,
upon seven years later.
Time had passed —
we were not the same.
I wished to hold back

the years
with my bare hands.

My heart had changed —
his had not.
I wanted to feel the same.
I manufactured the feelings.
We planned to meet,
but —
the call remained an idea.

Once he rang my doorbell.
He stood at the door expectantly.
"I just wanted to see you
and look at you," he said.
After he looked, he bolted away,
never to appear again.

Where are you, Sean?
I don't feel you on the earth.
Are you living in the heavens,
now,
looking down?
Why could you not have faced
yourself honestly?
Our synchronicity would
have helped us survive.

Our love was intense,
our attraction miraculous.
The rest could have been
faced and worked on.

Our seven-year itch.
"God,
was it Your design
that made us meet so often?
What were You saying to us?
That we were meant
to be together?"

If that be the case,
in seven years, seven upon
seven, seven million years,
let us meet and connect
in an "I" state,
our "not I" gone forever.

15

A Real Marriage

I resumed my relationship with Michael after my papa's death. We sought help as a couple from a woman therapist whom we also saw individually.

In my private sessions I sat in a chair opposite her, carving anxious hieroglyphics with my fingernails into the soft wood of her desk. I was not aware at that time just how much anxiety I felt about revealing myself to a woman. This anxiety was so great, it made me literally writhe in my chair. I was totally consumed by the memory of how often my mother had betrayed my confidence, how she would either punish me physically or reprimand me mercilessly about the information she deceitfully obtained. I could barely distinguish the difference between the therapist and the image of my mother as I sat before her, anxious and perspiring, keeping my hands occupied with a seemingly mindless task.

Years later the therapist asked me to observe the designs of the hieroglyphics I had sculpted into the side of her desk. To my astonishment they were crosses, vertical strokes intersected by horizontal ones. Some were encased in a square frame, some in two square frames, most free of borders; other crosses were scratched out, as though after drawing them I had wished to delete them.

At that later time, she asked me what the cross meant to me. I said it meant crucifixion. She asked if I was afraid of being crucified. I said yes.

I then realized with a dawning sense of awe that such was my inner state most of the time; that was how I experienced living in the world; that was what I expected from other people: crucifixion.

She told me that in the sessions when I felt confident and strong, she had watched me delete the crosses. On the other hand, when I felt overwhelmed by the world, I would draw new crosses or square frames around the crosses I had drawn before. The frames around the crosses seemed to mean I was immersed in the feeling of being crucified. The double frames seemed to mean I was so immersed in this feeling that, to my eyes, the world had become a dungeon in which I was being tortured with no respite. This is one of the few events I remember from my therapy with this woman. Despite the anguish I felt throughout the early stages of therapy, of whether or not to trust her, I persisted, because it brought relief to speak about my difficulties. Eventually, I began to look forward to every session with her.

The most memorable aspect of my first therapy dealt with my relationship with Michael. As I mentioned earlier, we both had individual sessions with her. He participated sporadically because he felt that I was the "sick" one, not he. I was hurt by his judgment, but I accepted it much as I had the judgment of my parents. I felt guilty about not loving him, not realizing at that time of my life that love could not be forced, and that his insistent need to extract love from me was equally "sick."

I, on the other hand, saw her as often as I could afford to, once and sometimes twice a week. I remember depriving myself of any unnecessary expenses. Sometimes I would cut down on my food and clothing expenses in order to pay for her help. Since my prideful nature was invested in owing money to no one, I always paid her promptly, no matter now serious the resulting deprivation. There was no doubt that therapy was an essential part of my life; I was like a lost dog that had found a juicy bone.

Michael and I conducted our relationship in the same way we always had. We did not live together, but saw one another whenever my busy dance schedule allowed. I danced professionally as often as jobs were available and, at the same time, rehearsed with artistic dance companies. Unfortunately, the artistic dance companies gave me no financial compensation. On tour, away from Michael, I would usually become involved with another male, who might or might not be married. I would engage with him sexually, be terribly excited by the adventure, then return to Michael like an innocent, chaste maiden.

He, however, was not waiting passively at home at this time of our involvement but was pursuing his needs with other women. Contrary to the nature of my clandestine affairs, he would speak openly about his other relationships, in order to threaten me and, without doubt, to validate whatever male strength he had acquired. No sooner was I aware of the other women than I would become desirous of his attention. When he succumbed to me, I would spurn him soon after.

We brought our problems to our mutual therapist, who would throw her hands into the air and advise that we separate. We could not. Since we could not leave one another, she suggested that we marry. This idea appealed to both of us.

We married in Mexico, taking the marital vows in a language neither of us understood. We nodded our heads solemnly and said "Sí" when the city clerk alerted us to do so by kicking our legs with his silver-gilded, heeled boot. We kissed lightly, not daring to look at each other, intent on remaining immersed in the unreal drama we had chosen for ourselves.

The city clerk and his assistants brought us to a cafe where we were sung to by four guitar players, drunk on tequila. The guitar players, in turn, insisted on bringing all of the guests in the cafe to our wedding table to wish us well. It was a buzzing, frivolous, merrymaking event in which we were toasted again and again. The music became more and more discordant as the players melted into alcoholic oblivion.

We, the bride and bridegroom, were also in an alcoholic euphoria from the constant toasting. We finally gave our adioses to whoever remained conscious, either slumped over the tables or lying on the floor. We went to our nuptial chamber and I, the bride, was suddenly overtaken by the desire to be really married, to feel totally committed to a man. I wanted all the cliche rituals of matrimony to be observed. I wanted to be carried over the threshold. I wanted to have a wedding night. I wanted. I wanted. I wanted. Where was all this excitement about the ritual of marriage coming from, I wondered.

I had bought a beautiful, lacy sleeping gown and I wanted to fuse with my bridegroom and become one for eternity. To become one for eternity. Was this an instinct like procreation, I wondered. If it was an instinct, it had been awakened by my "tequilaed" state, and I cajoled, purred, and stroked my bridegroom to get satisfaction. My bridegroom, however, was not harmonized in the same way; he was either too tired or, most likely, too angry at me, and all women, even to sleep with his bride in his arms. I did not weep. I simply stared into the darkness, feeling that I belonged to no one—least of all to myself.

In the morning I was deeply perturbed, not only by his rejection, but by my awakening desire to be united with a male. But I tucked it away in my unconscious, as I folded my unused, lacy sleeping outfit, to be returned to the department store when we arrived in America.

My untouched bridal nightgown proved symbolic of the aridity of our relationship. Finally, we both realized that it was time to part. Our therapist had suggested an unorthodox way to make us understand the futility of our alliance—a sticky, unhealthy, unbalanced alliance that had lasted too many years.

I had never been consciously aware of Michael's convoluted, poisoned connection to his mother. To her, he was a god. I had unconsciously intuited this aspect of his psychic disturbance, however, denying him the power he was always seeking from me: to be my god. Since the coercive, droning expression of his need paralleled the demands of my mother, which I had rejected all my life, our relationship was doomed from the beginning. My unconscious had turned him instantly into my mother, as my conditioned fear of her and the automatic, willful response to reject her demands took over my psyche. Because I was terrified to be alone in the world, I danced around him like a bear with its trainer, who dangled the honey. I, however, had the claws with which to destroy him. Emasculation of a man is a powerful claw.

When we arrived in America, not only did I return the lacy sleeping outfit to the department store, but I took off the marriage band my whispering knight had bought for the ceremony. I placed it alongside the diamond wedding band my papa had made. Within a year we divorced. I was once again free, free to search for the one, the right one, the one with whom I could fuse for eternity.

When I returned to my private session with my therapist and told her of our decision, she smiled: the severing of Michael's and my symbiotic connection had finally been accomplished. She asked me to join her in celebrating all the changes in my life over dinner. Afterward, I said a tearful, grateful farewell to her.

16

The Blue-Eyed Destroyer of the Dance

I moved to a new apartment. I painted the walls white and sanded the floors, making for myself a beautiful, safe nest. Even though my nest was beautiful and safe, I was racked with fear at the prospect of being alone. My whispering knight was physically out of my life, having left America to live in Europe. I felt the fear in the front part of my body, perceiving it like a gangplank for scurrying rats, looking for a safe corner in me in which to hide. This fear was constantly with me, even though I managed to hide its intensity while I engaged in the adventure of living.

I brought this feeling to my new male therapist, Dr. Roger Warner, a Bioenergetic psychiatrist, to whom I had been assigned by my first therapist. She wanted me to have the experience of a male therapist. She explained that because of my dance background, a Bioenergetic therapist, who dealt with the body as a mirror of the mind, would give me an important dimension of understanding that would benefit me greatly. Because it was a body therapy as well as an analytic therapy, he asked to see my physical condition. As he requested, I undressed—leaving on only my panties and brassiere. I was certain that he would find my body attractive and enticing. He scanned it thoroughly, asking me to bend, to stretch, to turn backwards, sidewards, and forward. He explained that this was customary in this type of therapy in order for the armoring of the body to become visible.

The image of a sultry sex symbol came to my mind as I gyrated accommodatingly before his bright, blue eyes. I felt overwhelmed by his vibrant energy and confidence, which slowly turned me into a little girl who wanted only to be acknowledged.

He was a sensitive, intuitive man, familiar with such machinations. He looked at me kindly and said that if I were truly comfortable in my body, I would not be putting on a display of sexuality. He suggested I feel the fear that was in my body, which would help me stay connected to myself in a truthful way.

I put on my clothes, bewildered by his statements, wondering why I should wish to feel the fear in my body, a feeling that awakened me during the night with a frozen scream caught in my throat, a scream I could not release.

He saw the question in my eyes and told me that releasing the fear inside me was the only way I could regain the mobility of my body. Since I had the agility of a dancer, I refused to believe that he was referring to me. I was certain he thought my body beautiful, lithe, graceful, and desirable.

I was shocked when I heard his diagnosis: stiff, frozen, and unexpressive. I blurted out, close to tears, that I was considered the most expressive dancer in my field. He looked at me again with his steady, blue-eyed gaze: "In that case, the field must consist of more frozen, stiffer bodies than yours." I felt overwhelmed by his directness. Nevertheless I made another appointment, not certain I would keep it.

His statements kept buzzing in my head as I took dance classes, observing other dancers and their agility or lack of it. No matter what his point of view about my body might be, I was intent during the week before my next session to prove him wrong. Among the other dancers I received accolades as never before for my beauty of movement. I intended to tell the blue-eyed destroyer of the dance that he was a charlatan. Honest expression was still difficult for me, but I mobilized myself to resist any other critical comments he might make.

He greeted me at the door, shaking my hand energetically, and ushered me into his office with so much concern and interest that I lost my resolve. I sat in a chair opposite him, silent, masked and terrified.

He asked me if the previous session had upset me. I told him that it had not, that I knew my field better than he did, and that if he were to see me perform, he would alter his opinion about the stiffness and unexpressiveness of my body.

He remained quiet for a few seconds, then jumped up from his chair and left the room as he instructed me to undress. I had decided beforehand never to let him see me unclothed again, even though I understood that taking off most of one's clothing was the best way a patient's body could be observed and worked with in this particular therapy. His brisk, decisive manner once again broke my resolve; I consented, with the intent of proving to myself that he could no longer affect me. When he returned I stood before him in my brassiere and underwear.

He eyed me quickly, looked at my body, said, "Ahuh" and told me to go over the breathing stool.

"What?" I asked.

He pointed to a two-foot-high stool onto which were piled and fastened two rolled blankets. "The breathing stool."

I laughed defiantly as I approached this contraption, which I later referred to as "the rack." I mirthfully told him that I did not hear it breathe. His bright, blue eyes turned a darker blue, imparting the sense of an impending storm. He restrained his irritation, however, and gently guided me to the stool. He explained that arching my back over the rolled blankets on the stool would elicit deep breathing that would change my body.

I thought, "Hah! Change *my* body? Impossible. It's perfect."

One would have assumed that arching over rolled blankets would be soothing, easy to do. To my dismay, the attempt to breathe made me cough, sometimes choke, and resist breathing even more by holding my muscles tighter. I felt as though I were lying on jagged rocks that were pressing into my back, causing unbearable pain. When I attempted to breathe, I experienced the front of my body to be so tight that I had the impression of being suspended on a rack, pulled limb from limb.

When he saw my reaction, he voiced another "Ahuh." He asked if I wanted to get up from the stool.

"No," I said, intent on proving that I could breathe freely. I tried to breathe, but could not.

"You are holding your breath," he said quietly.

"No, I am not," I gasped.

He asked if I would like to breathe more freely. With another defiant laugh, I dared him to have me do so. He ignored my reaction this time and palpated my neck and jaw muscles, digging deeply into the frozen musculature with his knuckles. This elicited so much pain that I was forced to breathe, screaming in agony. I crumpled to the floor, sobbing.

He held my hand while I slowly found my way back to reality. I was dumbfounded at the hidden terror I had experienced, how once again I had emotionally been pulled back into the cellar into which my papa had forced me at the age of three. Dr. Warner explained that the terror of this event was still hidden in the musculature of my body, creating stiffness and therefore lack of movement and expression.

I suddenly understood that despite my contracted musculature, I was still an expressive, beautiful dancer. But how much more would this be true without the armoring! He congratulated me upon my quick perception of the situation and my willingness to undergo more unthawing. I was again astounded by his confident assumption that I would wish to continue this torturous process. When he asked me how I felt, I admitted that I felt less stiff, freer, and more emotionally available. He beamed at my response and shook my hand again as I left his office. I returned to my apartment, canceled all appointments and slept for the rest of the day.

When I awakened twenty-four hours later, I felt as though I had been shot out of a cannon and released into a new dimension. I did indeed feel freer and closer to real feelings. I became committed to the new process and to my new "guru."

I came to my next session less resistant, more willing to make myself available to the therapy, though with trepidation. Dr. Warner sensed that the previous session had been traumatic for me and assured me that not every session would have so severe an effect. He gradually became acquainted with my history as we concentrated on releasing the frozen musculature. He intuited my basic nature: my sensitivity, my artistry, my unworldliness. He also sensed that underneath my frozen muscles seethed rage and deep misery. He worked slowly and gently with me and, as time passed, I felt my body differently.

I began to understand more clearly his initial reaction to my frozen stiffness. I began to understand as I became less frozen how contracted other dancers' bodies were. I began to understand that my field consisted of many frozen, contracted people who had the potential of becoming either physically ill or psychiatric cases, if they did not avail themselves of an activity like dance that forced them to breathe. Dr. Warner pointed out to me that an organism needs an outlet for feelings and expression or it atrophies: the less one breathes, the more distorted and often mentally disturbed one becomes.

I was struck by the fact that the expressive aspect of the dance had been influenced and even determined by the frozen people in this field, having an incalculably damaging effect on the art form. I began to understand that because I had frozen my feelings and my body in order to protect myself against my parents, I no longer lived in my body; I no longer inhabited it. I visited my body like a furnished room to which I would come from time to time to have sex or to gaze upon it narcissistically, as before the mirrors of dance studios. I, as well as the dance world, referred to the body as an "instrument." An instrument is meant to be manipulated, to be shaped into a particular form. Most important, it must be devoid of humanness.

17

I Hate Her, I Hate Her

D r. Warner asked me in one of my sessions to express anger at my
mother. To my astonishment I could not. I was astonished because I
was aware that I had been filled with anger at this woman for my entire
life.

He placed me before a bed with my arms in clenched fists, stretched
behind my shoulders and head. He asked me to imagine my mother on the
bed and to hit her. I assumed the posture, thinking it would be easy; it
reminded me of a Flamenco dancer's. When he instructed me to breathe
in this position, however, and to jut out my lower jaw in a gesture of
defiance, then hit the imaginary figure of my mother on the bed, my body
became frozen. My eyes darted back and forth, wild with terror. I backed
away from the bed, collapsing helplessly on a chair, looking at my
therapist as though he were an executioner. I went behind my eyes.

He took my hands to bring me back to reality and said, "It's not so
easy, is it?"

I felt bewildered. I knew I hated my mother, yet I could not express
the feeling. My terror of her had become frozen into my body. My psyche,
meanwhile, had disengaged from the terror as though it were not real. I
began to understand how one can live one's life with an "as if" reality,
making gestures about living but never embodying life nor feeling it.

I shook my head as though speaking to myself. My last insight had invigorated me. I looked at Dr. Warner with renewed determination, went to the bed, and assumed the Flamenco posture. "Now what?" His blue eyes sparkled excitedly as he stood by me, ready for more transformation.

Once again, he told me to look at the image of my mother on the bed and tell her, "I hate you." He instructed me to strike her with clenched fists.

Challenged in the deepest part of my will, I made the effort to move from the Flamenco posture, in which I had been locked for almost a minute, and begin hitting the image on the bed.

To my chagrin I could not move my back from the arched position to the rounded position which my spine would have assumed had I hit the object, my mother. He shouted encouragingly to me to hit her, to scream out my hatred of her, but I could not move from the Flamenco posture.

I was in a state of panic, questioning myself silently about what was happening to my body. I remained mute and frozen, a study of willfulness, pride, and fear. Dr. Warner realized that my back had gone into spasm because the terror of expressing such feelings to my mother had paralyzed my body. He gently palpated the spastic muscles until I was able to move out of the arched position and bend forward. I touched the floor with my fingertips, keeping my legs in a bent, grounded position to stabilize the energy and the feelings.

While in this position, my head to the ground, my focus away from him, I realized that I felt hopeless. I was so ashamed of my inability to perform this seemingly simple movement that I wished to melt into the floor. I wondered how I, an expert dancer, one who had received acclaim from audiences and teachers, could find herself in such humiliating, defeating circumstances.

My therapist, sensing my consternation, helped me rise from the grounding position to an upright one in which I still maintained a grounded stance; that is, one in which I stayed in contact with the floor by keeping my thigh joints, legs, and ankles bent so as to remain in contact not only with the floor, but also with my body. He stood before me, looking deeply into my eyes. I sensed his compassion and understanding; I relinquished my prideful will and fell into his arms, sobbing.

He held me until I regained my composure. Reduced to a three-year-old child, I murmured on his chest that I was a failure, but I would show him. I would perform better the next time. He drew me away from him and said, "It's a deal!"

I returned to his office, intent on giving the best performance of my life. I had practiced the Flamenco posture in front of my mirror and had interrogated Spanish dancers about the proper positioning of the body in this form of dance. I was ready to excel and to demonstrate my excellence. He noticed my willingness to go to the bed and show him I had been rehearsing the Flamenco posture, but he diverted me from doing so. Instead, he took me by the hands and guided me to a chair opposite his. He gently informed me that I was not auditioning to be an acceptable candidate for therapy but that I was there to express the repressed feelings in my system: for the moment, toward my mother. He told me the form into which he had placed my body was important only to the extent that it would elicit breathing and feelings, and that I was not being observed by an audience.

I felt embarrassed. He then asked me what my feelings were toward my mother. I told him quickly that I hated her. He made me aware that I was mentally clear about my feelings but still unable to express them emotionally and physically.

He suggested I express this hatred of her in dance movements. I could not. He explained that I was so traumatized by these feelings that not even with a dance phrase, a form of expression familiar to me, could I release the dreaded feelings.

I sat back in my chair and looked at him pleadingly. My eyes begged him silently not to denigrate me further. He understood and explained that the purpose of his work with me was for me to reclaim the repressed feelings in my psyche, which would enable me to reclaim a more expressive body and become a whole person.

My enthusiasm was rekindled by his words because I wanted all of it: to be more expressive and to be whole. He explained, as he led me back to the bed, that the only way the repressed feelings could be coaxed to the surface was to make the effort to express them — no matter how adequately or inadequately they emerged. He tried to impress upon me that there would be no judgment or criticism about the matter, that his office was not like my former household, filled with brutality and denigration, nor was it like the highly critical, competitive dance world. I was convinced.

Dr. Warner placed a tennis racket in my hands. The racket would intensify the stretch of my arms behind my head and shoulders, thus eliciting deeper breathing. Once again he told me to visualize my mother on the bed and to scream out my hatred of her.

I opened my mouth, but no sound came. My throat was tight, my jaws were locked, and my mouth would not open beyond a slit. He shouted to me to try again. I tried again to open my mouth wider; it opened further, but still no sound emerged from this aperture that now felt like an exposed cave. He screamed insistently at me to make a sound, any sound.

I tried repeatedly until a whispering screech could be heard, resembling the croak of a frog submerged in the thickets. Dr. Warner quickly palpated my neck muscles until I was forced to scream. As I did so, I hit the bed with the tennis racket while I bellowed forth, this time with an elephant's indignant, trumpeting cry, that I hated her, I hated her, I hated her. I hit and hit and hit and screamed until my body and voice were exhausted.

I felt as though I had been plummeted into an ancient cavern fathoms below the ground, hurling a pick against a hard, encrusted surface until I finally broke through. Little by little, my Mona Lisa sideways smile gave way to a rageful, menacing expression. It contained the fury and contempt that had been frozen into my face for as long as I had lived in that household.

Red in the face, still enraged and breathing heavily, I threw the racket on the bed and grounded my legs and body. I was in my body as never before. My focus was within me. I was not aware of the therapist. I was in touch with my feelings. I had finally experienced an "I."

As my breathing became normal, Dr. Warner came to me, shook my hand and said, "All right! All right!" He then left the room while I dressed. I did not need his farewells.

My gait was strong and confident as I approached the street and life. I looked around me, daring anyone to challenge me. My body felt tall enough that I might touch the sky with my head. From this height and from my groundedness, I felt I could look at the throng and confront any challenger.

Those feelings lasted for a few days, but gradually my customary energy returned. I had experienced my rage, however, and this experience would not soon be forgotten. I had become aware of its ferocity and its energy. My rage became less of a mystery to me, and therefore less awesome.

I needed to repeat this energetic action with my guru in his office before my assertion would become an intrinsic part of my psyche. As my sessions with my guru continued, I noticed a monumental change in my psyche in that I became less fearful of others, consequently less of a target for their abuse.

I grounded my energy while in Dr. Warner's sessions. I also accustomed myself to ground my energy before a performance, which unified my body and psyche. The feeling of unity achieved from grounding my body gave me a stronger sense of self from which I danced more confidently and more expressively. I functioned from this unity as a human being. I relied upon this tool; it became as much second nature as brushing my teeth.

As time passed, I noticed that my feet, which had high insteps and high arches, giving them a gazelle-like look, now were flatter and closer to the ground. I had become known for that arched look: other dancers gazed enviously upon those structured appendages. Little had I realized, or would my admirers ever suspect, that that look had been created by the most severe tension, not only in the feet, but in the rest of the body. Being armored in the body pulled my weight off my feet. I was not on the earth. I was disconnected, therefore a solely mental being, functioning from an image of myself instead of the real feelings that comprised the real me.

I was shocked to learn this truth, but I did not resist it, for it rang true in every cell of my being. I embraced it totally and slowly the gazelle became more of a terrestrial creature. I remember being concerned about the look of my feet not only because it changed my ethereal image, but because my feet became two sizes larger. Finding shoes to fit them became increasingly a problem.

Dance is a poetic art form. Since I was innately poetic, I had felt at home in it. The changes that occurred in my body, therefore, were of great concern. My feet grew bigger, my abdomen more expanded; because I was breathing more freely, my entire frame became larger.

I realized that in the contracted "not I" state, which had been my familiar stance in life as well as in the dance, an expansive body was cause for anxiety, if not alarm. I became aware that one's neurotic and/or psychotic contracted self lent itself well to the dance training because this training was the antithesis of normal breathing; flowing, free movements; uncontracted buttocks, abdomen, and feet. It was the antithesis of human expression.

I began to understand the constraints that had been put upon dancers' bodies by training. Because I was discovering my real body, I finally experienced the real joy of movement. I was no longer only an ethereal creature, but a dancing woman in a grounded reality. My body was no longer an "instrument," but a part of who I was becoming.

18

Changing: Evolving an "I"

It is a peculiar state, like a thawing out.
It is a variegated garden with some flowers
and some weeds.
When I was "not I,"
I glided on the earth,
with no eyes to see, no ears to hear,
no voice to speak from,
and no breath to breathe.

I had been the zero of the Tarot card,
called the Fool, or
the "dumkopf," as my mother would say.
And now, the zero could become one,
two, three to ten.
After ten I can become double me to 11, 12, 13.
I can keep adding to myself until
I can become three billion,
if I wish.

I am approaching an "I."
My heart and body are thawing out.

My heart is pink, small, and tight as yet.
It has tolerance, but not for much as yet:
myself, my cats, my friends, my struggles,
my therapist, my work.

Has my heart kindness
to spare for the world?
Not too much.
It is too vast a place,
too reminiscent of "them."
But "they" are fading into the past,
like two toothless crocodiles
that no longer bite one another,
or me.

The wounds are healing, but slowly.
New wounds are being inflicted,
by others and the world.
These fresh wounds heal faster
because my perceptions are
clearer.

In this new state I can become known,
I might become rich,
I might be coddled,
I might be kicked.
But neither "they" nor the world
can knock down the gate to my heart,
causing me to lie like a
struggling bug on its back,
unable to turn right-side up.

I, too, am learning to lash out,
to reach for what I want.

I'm here on this earth to learn its ways.
I incorporate these ways,
even though they might grate.

Here is my "I."
Do you like it?
You do?
That is good!
If not, that's too bad.
I'm here just like you.
I'll not shrink away
when you come closer to me.
Let's look at each other
with deep curiosity.

As my heart opens fully,
I'll reach toward you more.
I'll know who you are,
and embrace you in truth.

19

The Outsider

My process was truly a "thawing out." I had named it correctly. Little by little, I regained my body, therefore I reclaimed my feelings, and, therefore, an identity other than a dancer. It was not an easy process. Often my world was turned upside down. The values I had been living from were no longer workable.

That was most apparent in my field. Dance was my profession and my livelihood. I had questioned many aspects of the dance world and its training of dancers long before I had been exposed to my guru's therapy. I remember going to dance concerts wishing to be moved by the performance and the performers. Invariably I was disappointed. While the audience was applauding and cheering, I sat unmoved. Critics wrote glowing reviews the day following the performance, which made me think that I was crazy. I never understood while in my "not I" state why I remained unmoved; I simply felt like an outsider who had never been acknowledged for my differences. I could never accept their values. I continued functioning in my field, however, though agonized and frustrated.

Finally my questions about my dissatisfaction with my field were answered through the therapy with my guru and corroborated by the unthawing of my body and psyche. I had been looking for a truer connection to my body and therefore myself, one which would make all expression truthful and beautiful. Now I had found it. My guru confirmed these feelings and I finally realized that my search was not pathological. I understood as never before that the training of the dancers and the world of dance in general were antithetical to a healthy, breathing, feeling body and psyche. I was overjoyed that I had finally found some answers to my dissatisfaction. I now had to face my world and try to live in it with a sense of truth.

When I was not engaged in Broadway shows, I earned my living teaching dance for organizations or schools set up for that purpose. I had gained a great deal of popularity as a teacher; my classes were filled to overflowing. Each class was like a performance for me and the students. I received thunderous applause after each class. This bolstered my "I" state considerably, making me aware of my accomplishments.

As my unthawing continued, however, I found I could not teach with the same fervor or the same conviction. I wanted to apply to the dance some of the concepts I was involved with. As a consequence, I began to speak about grounding, breathing, expanded abdomens, uncontracted buttocks, and feeling the movement.

I knew my ideas were unorthodox, but I could not restrain myself. I was no longer tolerant of the mechanical quality of the students' movements, of their superficial connection to their bodies. I remember my first experimental class in which some of my new concepts were applied. The students had come into the class as usual, expecting a command performance. Instead, I asked them to experience their bodies, feel them, and express their feelings accordingly.

I experimented with breathing while they sat on each others' bodies to elicit breathing. I sometimes kept them in a plié, or bent position of the legs, in order to ground them, hoping they would experience their legs and bodies in more dynamic ways. They would scream with pain as they felt the amount of contraction they had accumulated to keep their bodies in a feelingless state. I encouraged them to breathe into their pain, to let go to the ground. The moans, groans, and shouts of the students brought the school authorities to the studio door. They stood, looked on quizzically, then dashed away.

Nothing was said to me, so I continued with my new-found interest. The reactions of the students varied from tittering nervously to yawning to confused, hidden anger. A few were interested. In time, the classes dwindled to those select few, who sensed that new ideas were brewing and who were courageous and curious enough to experiment with me.

Most of the students were baffled by my new direction. They spoke about it to the other teachers and the authorities of the school. All were confused by my point of view, particularly since it was completely opposed to the teachings of the other instructors and the dance field at large. I continued with excitement and vigor to teach my classes using Bioenergetic concepts.

One day, however, as I entered the studio for my appointed class at the appointed time, I was shocked to find no students. I sat in my customary seat, waiting. I remained in my chair until it became uncomfortably clear that I was alone, that my ideas had been rejected by the students, and that I would most likely be fired.

When I left the school, no one was at the desk, making it impossible for me to get their reaction to my work. I felt very much alone with my convictions, felt a mixture of defiance, betrayal, and terror. These feelings were not new to me, but at that moment I did not realize that. As I walked home I was almost faint with humiliation and terror.

Several days after the humiliating event, I received a letter, explaining that my classes had fallen below the accepted attendance level. If I wished to experiment in such radical ways I should find a position that lent itself better to such experimentation. They also said they would be interested in taking me back should I retrieve my former sensibilities and reenter the fold.

I was devastated. I took the letter to my guru, who advised me to find other work and to start my own dance company. He was not perturbed by my dismissal because he too was a maverick in his field. Functioning alone in uncharted territory was not unfamiliar to him. I was heartened by his support and his example of pioneer energy.

I started my own dance company. I trained my dancers with Bio-energetic concepts. In time, I developed dancers who thought as I did and who personally opened themselves to Bioenergetic therapy. We became a unified group, espousing the same cause.

From this unanimity, I created dance pieces which were eventually performed publicly. My dancers had round bellies, grounded feet and legs. They expressed their feelings through their movements; they loved to move, were full-bodied beings.

My pieces dealt with the psychological evolution of a woman in search of her female self and the processes she needed to undergo in order to love the male and be united with him. On the stage, I depicted frustration, schizophrenia, rage, tears, play, womanliness, and, ultimately, the unity of the male and female.

My guru was involved with developing my performance concepts. Together, we unconsciously became a coalition to revolutionize the dance world and bring more truth to it. It was an exciting time for both of us. He was pioneering his work in the psychological world as I was doing in mine. He was paving his way in a rigidified Freudian modality by bringing body concepts into it. I was trying to make an inroad into my field by devising healthier concepts of the body, expressive movements and more meaningful, artistic statements.

At his request, I demonstrated the body tools he used in his work at lectures and seminars. At such events I was witness to the almost violent opposition of other therapists to his work. I was witness to how my guru stood up to such opponents. I saw how, in the face of some of the enraged opposition he received from the therapists, he mobilized his energy. I noticed it course rapidly from the heels of his feet through his vertebral column to the top of his head and forehead into his eyes. He was in complete control at such times, his blue eyes piercing laser-like at them. Invariably, they would withdraw, as though struck by lightning, and drop grudgingly into their seats.

Whenever I was witness to such reactions, I grew more deeply impressed by his conviction and power. I wanted such power. I wanted such conviction. I wanted such strength. I adored, admired, respected, and worshiped this man. My transference to him was complete. I was locked into it totally. He could do no wrong.

Are you the one I can emulate?
Are you someone who can
make me feel real?
Not forever.
Just for a little while.

Without mirroring you,
I'll never be me.
My "I" will remain nebulous —
too much like my "not I."

Let me bring my "I" to yours,
to experience if it fits.
This is not stealing.
You must believe me.

I would not recognize your "I,"
if the same were not in me.
You are part of my "I"
as I am part of yours.
Therefore, let me taste it,
savor yours while it blends with mine.
For are we all not fused like this
with our God,
who made us first?

Had I been your beloved child,
you would have loved this part of me,
whose "I" connects to yours.

You would have seen yourself in me
as I see myself in you.
If you must loathe me,
as a result of this exchange,

your loathing is your own self-hate,
showing you its face,
becoming our shared state.

Let me emulate you.
Give me your go-ahead.
It will not be long before
my own energy
comes to the fore —
powerful, strong, courageous,
not as you, but as me.

Yours has triggered mine.
Is this not how the universe
hangs together,
beginning with God's grace,
passed on to all?

20

Transference

I gobbled up my guru's professional "I." I wanted it for myself and in myself. I understand now that the qualities I admired in him were always in me. If they had not been, I would never have recognized them in him, would not have wished to devour them in him, devour him.

As I continued to thaw out, I discovered I needed a male to emulate. My guru became that male energy for me. I absorbed his aggression, his assertion, his authority in his work. I gobbled up his creativity in his field, even though his field was different from mine. I gobbled up his integrity about life. However, I never desired nor was attracted to his phallicism, his sexual self, about which he was very prideful. This lack of chemistry bewildered me. Once again I doubted the validity of my perceptions about his maleness.

However, my lack of sexual attraction to him did not obstruct his overall positive imprint on me. Since there had been no one else in my life whom I could mirror in a positive way, and since his imagery was so dynamic for me, I absorbed and affirmed all of it. When I watched him in public, I looked upon him with the awe and admiration of a child watching a magic show. I looked at him in seminars with my enigmatic, sideways glance smacking of total possession, even though I knew he was very much a married man.

When he lectured, his gaze would occasionally rest upon me. My heart would snap to attention while I blushed a vivid red. I would nod my head to give him the approval I thought he needed as he spoke. I wanted to smother him with every ounce of devotion, respect, and adoration I could muster in this subtle exchange between us. I would look around at the audience, detecting any opponents to his ideas. I envisioned myself, sword in hand, confronting such bedeviled beings.

The seminars generally occurred after long work days. I sensed his fatigue. I wished to refresh him by bathing his face in a scented cloth, to relieve his tension. At the end of these meetings, I gazed at him indirectly, stole quietly to his side and whispered an overwhelmed goodnight. He would invariably be surrounded by people. Should he not acknowledge my timid, heartfelt farewell, I would walk home in great agony.

But such agony was counteracted by the greater consciousness I had gained in my therapy. My ego had become markedly stronger than when in my "not I" state. I approached the issue of being overlooked or of possible rejection in a more logical, less pained way. Nevertheless, I was still dramatically involved in my dynamic transference to him. I would review my participation in the seminar; if I discovered that my questions or answers had been less than brilliant, I thoroughly studied the subject matter under discussion, altered my understanding and attempted to be brilliant the next time.

To change my awkward feelings when in his presence, I decided to call him by his first name like everyone else. I had, until now, addressed my guru as Dr. Warner, distancing me from the reality of him; it served to keep him on the pedestal I had created. I practiced a more relaxed attitude in his presence by not focusing my attention upon him and by being more conversational with the other members. I would deliberately initiate a conversation with another male so my guru would know that other men appealed to me also. I ceased whispering my farewells to him and left the meetings with the others. I felt audacious in these efforts. But my heart remained agitatedly focused on him.

After some weeks of my new maneuvers, he approached me to assist him in a workshop. I was convinced that my scheming had been successful. I felt I had finally mastered a way to deal with my awkward, unclear feelings toward this god.

I gave him an enthusiastic "yes." But when he casually asked if I had attended the last seminar, I felt as though I were again drowning in my own muck. I realized that he had not even known I was present. I could not believe he had not seen me there. I returned to my apartment, wondering if I were crazy.

I began to question my obsession toward him. I wondered about my stilted manner in his presence, my shyness, my inability to be more forthright, more myself. I wanted to function from the same self in his office and in seminars as I did in the outside world. The truth was that I became mute when I needed to address him directly. He had the habit of pushing away whatever or whomever he did not want with a flick of the fingers of his right hand. Over the ten years, I had watched this gesture exile several people, and I dreaded it as I would the blade of a guillotine.

I never openly remonstrated, "You are hurting me, ignoring me, using me, not giving me my due." Instead, I would cling more tenaciously, lending myself to whatever negative reactions he might or might not have to my hypersensitive, persistent possession of him. Try as I might, I could not be free with him. Instead, I confronted a wall, thousands of feet thick, against which I would bang my head, along which I would scamper like a frantic mouse, looking for an opening to the other side.

I was trapped in these feelings toward my guru and essentially toward all men. I remained in a circular whirl, getting relief from my secret musings by deciding to become more appealing, more intelligent, and more schooled.

Some of my efforts he noticed and commented on. But, because I was unable to address the real issue, that of my possessive transference, my psyche was caught in spinning similar webs as I had with my papa. The nature of the webs with my guru was vastly more complex and painful, because I was more conscious of my motivation. My efforts to extricate myself from this maze of confused feelings was exhausting, often making me feel crazy, inadequate and perpetually frustrated. I was convinced I would never get what I wanted from him, from any man, from my papa. I remained the mouse on the treadmill.

I became tired, tired of my obsessive thoughts about him, of the unnatural, willful patterns I had established in order to relate to him. I longed for a miraculous reprieve from the pain and confusion of the transference. No reprieve came. Instead, I continued my charade. My personal relationship with him was never addressed, by him or me. I remained his golden-haired little princess, by whom he was admired, respected and loved.

21

An Empty Heart

Then I met Ivan, a tall, stocky man, in the seminar. He was a chiropractor, searching for his personal identity as well as his professional one. Because he was extremely talented in his work and restlessly searching for a deeper way to work with the body, he found the seminars exciting and fulfilling. They answered some of the questions he had been asking for a lifetime. Like me, he wanted to expand his vision, to expand his inner horizon as well. He was not particularly handsome, but his energy was compelling and charismatic.

Our shared interests became even more intense when he involved himself with a Bioenergetic therapist. We shared every nuance of our feelings, our latest psychological discoveries, my dance issues, his work problems. It was a sharing I had never experienced before, heightened by a passionate, exciting, sexual exchange.

I could not believe that such a connection was possible; I savored every moment of it, wanting a child and marriage. He was in the process of divorcing; my desires were acknowledged, but needed to wait.

He was supportive of my dance concepts, which had evolved since my therapeutic work with my guru, and came to all my dance concerts. He applauded my performances enthusiastically, giving expert criticism. He helped teach the students in my studio, using his chiropractic knowledge, applying an innate healing ability to the work that was appreciated by all.

He lent excitement to our work together, to our holistic alliance. However, we did not have enough time to explore our discoveries, our theories, with each other.

We attended Dr. Warner's seminars. Ivan would sit with his arm around my shoulders, holding my hand. I thought I saw my guru wince as he observed our closeness and turned away. I felt squeamish at being seen in public in this intimate position. At the same time, I relished having a male counterpart. As soon as I saw my guru turn away, I saw with my mind's eye an image of my papa with his arm around my mamma's shoulder. They too were holding hands. I, then ten years old, looked at them forlornly, just a seat away, wanting desperately to be touched, to be part of them. Instead, I felt I was a stranger, out in the cold, fending for myself.

On the one hand I felt embarrassed and anxious that I was living in a more fulfilled way, but I was also experiencing being close to a man, no longer looking enviously and longingly at others with such fulfillment. "Will my guru accept that I am in a relationship of my own?" I wondered. "He will have to," was my immediate response. "After all, is not one of the purposes of therapy to find a satisfying partner?" I wanted to stick my tongue out at him and say, "So there! I can have my own man! Who needs you anymore?"

After my lover and I attended several seminars, my guru suddenly suggested that I stop coming to them. I acquiesced to his desire as one imposed by a monarch whose deified nature could never be questioned. I do not recall asking him for an explanation. Nor was one offered! I no longer attended the seminars, though I avidly asked Ivan about them, as he did continue to attend. The only explanation I could give myself about my guru's perplexing decision was a deeply unconscious one: that he was secretly involved with me, much like my papa, and could not tolerate another man in my life. This explanation gave me solace; in many ways it served to create the feeling of being loved, a love insinuated, not acknowledged.

For the first year Ivan's and my relationship had a honeymoon quality. Soon after, however, Ivan decided that he no longer wanted to continue in the chiropractic field. He began searching intensely for where he belonged. His restlessness put a strain on our connection. He became withdrawn, occupied with his search, spending hours meeting with others who seemed more realized. When he returned home, he was unwilling to share himself with me in any way, but locked himself in his room, ostensibly to work out his dilemma.

During our time together, I had found within myself a giving, loving, full-bodied nature: I became aware of some of the real, feminine qualities I possessed. Heretofore, I had never been able to express these aspects of myself. I therefore yearned for more consistency in the relationship, to further explore this female self that had been emerging. When he withdrew from me, I became the monstrous image of my mother: demanding, sexually insistent, intolerant of his plight.

The more I plagued him to satisfy my needs, the more he withdrew, until our golden year of bliss receded into shadows. The magical attraction between us faded away, like a mythical event that had occurred eons of time ago. We became wanderers in our parents' labyrinth, expressing ourselves from their hateful confusion, destroying any valid moment between us.

One day, as a result of a demanding episode on my part, he took a wooden bowl from the table and crushed it with his hands before my eyes, then stomped on it. I realized the object symbolized me.

To my surprise I did not faint, nor did I shrink away, as I might have earlier in my life. Instead, I took another bowl from the table, stood on a chair to match his height, and bashed it on his head. We looked at one another in amazement; then we laughed until we were exhausted. We held one another and had our last serious talk. We decided that a separation was necessary, that time and space might heal our rupture. We would remain open for a possible future alliance.

I told my guru of our violent exchange. He intimated that the relationship was "bad" for me. I remembered the sexual appetite Ivan and I had for one another, the sharing of our individual and unique ideas, the consuming involvement. Moreover, Ivan had become an important teacher in my studio. I knew he would be missed. I thought of the healing energy of his hands, how distraught I would be at its absence.

I wondered, "How can Ivan be 'bad' for me?" Nevertheless, I listened to my guru's admonition, realizing that it was unlike him to be so candid with me.

Ivan and I moved apart, but still lived on the same block. I would watch him pass my apartment building. He would look up at my window. We would wave to one another. Sometimes he would come to my door and I would let him in. We would enjoy each other's body. He would dress and leave. I felt I would go mad until the next encounter. I did not wish to make demands on him, but I could not restrain myself. He would instantly withdraw.

Dr. Warner heard my pain and encouraged me to stay away from Ivan. Sometimes I could do so, feeling stronger for it. But, not long after my guru's repeated advice, my lover would appear at the door, ready to consummate his sexual desire for me. I would submit to him with little hesitation. Again, he would dress and leave. Again, I felt I would go mad.

Dr. Warner threatened to stop therapy with me if I continued to see him. "My guru is trying to help me," I thought. "I must do what he advises." But I could not, nor could Ivan. We were devastatingly attracted to one another and we could not do without the other. In the long run, however, Ivan was not ready for a committed relationship.

One day, as I agonized about my connection to Ivan, I asked myself, "Am *I* ready?" I answered, "I'm readier by far than he. If I stay with Ivan, I'll never find out to what extent I will be able to relate to a man."

I wanted to go beyond where we were. I wanted to find out if I could truly love a man. I asked, "God, why do my relationships always abort? What is wrong? What is wrong with me?"

Ivan left for Europe — as had Michael, my whispering knight. I returned to my guru's fold, back to his feet. I could see that he needed my adoration, much as he had needed the adoration his mother had given him throughout his life. I forgave him for that need, in the same way I had forgiven my papa. "They are human" was my rationalization. I continued to move in their shadows.

My pattern was broken by an invitation to teach dance in Israel. Dr. Warner urged me to accept it. Since I was eager to leave the old environment, with its memories of lost loves and dance frustrations, I made plans for the new adventure.

I had also been receiving pleading telephone calls from Ivan from abroad, to meet him and marry him. Tongue in cheek, I consented, making plans to stop overnight in Zurich, Switzerland, en route to my final destination. I did not really envision marrying him, but I was intrigued by his desire and by being wanted. Finally I would be in a position to say "no" to a man.

To my chagrin Ivan was not at the airport as we had arranged. I went to a hotel, defeated.

Several hours later, he appeared in the lobby of my hotel. I had taken a single room for the night, since my flight was scheduled for the next morning. How he had discovered my whereabouts puzzles me to this day. When we saw one another, we embraced briefly, and after a cursory glance into my eyes, he steered me toward my room. Nothing was said. Our passion for one another was living still. I drowned out my shrieking inner voices and listened only to the untamed lust of my body. I surrendered totally as our sexuality ignited. My now-permissive conscience whispered conspiringly, "Just one more time. It will be the last time."

Our passion consummated, our tryst was interrupted by the manager of the hotel. She knocked on the door of my room, opened it, sniffing the air disapprovingly as she eyed the disarray around my single bed. She told us that a single occupant had no right to have a visitor in the room. I assured her that this rule was unknown by me and did not exist in American hotels. She left, after telling Ivan that he must leave immediately.

We left the hotel soon after her unpleasant warning and ate in a small restaurant, drank the vintage wine of the region and listened to one another in the time I had left to catch my plane for the Middle East.

As I listened to his stories of confusion, poverty, and search, I wonderingly remembered his insistent pleas for marriage in his phone calls to me in America. I felt both pity and repulsion for him and his confusion about his life, especially when he asked me, like a beggar, for my Swiss francs, which I could not exchange. I gave him all my small change as he expostulated about our future marriage on his and my return to the United States.

We embraced. I walked away from him as though from a stranger. I entered the plane. By the time I was seated, he had disappeared from view. I still felt his healing touch on my body, but I had somehow finally let go of him.

I wondered quietly how much of my mother was operating in me at this point. I did not understand yet the concept of Reflectivism — that I came into this life with her qualities. This awareness needed much probing, but I had much more to endure before the concept could be accepted by me.

22

Have a Heart

Hot, hot genitals.
Passion —
split off from the heart.
"I've got to have it.
You! Come here.
Serve me, enter me,
make yourself available.
Move till ecstasy comes."

Then, what?
A satiated body!
Two beings looking at
each other —
filled, but empty.
"Oh, yes!
What did you say your name was?"
"Anneliese."
"Yes, I remember.
I'll see you when I feel
like this again."

"Do you love me?"
I ask anxiously.
"What do you think?"
he questions.
"I hope you do,"
I answer plaintively.

Unsatisfied, still yearning,
wanting more, more,
and more.
"You never get enough,"
he says, annoyed.
"Look!
I'm getting hard again."
"That's good,"
I assure him,
"but don't you feel more,
elsewhere?"

"You want me to say
I love you?"
he asks,
on the verge of
hysterical laughter.
"Yes," I answer.
"Why not?
It would give me completion."

"You want too much!"
he bellows forth, accusingly.
"Is it too much to let me know
you love me?
It's so good to be with you.
So special, this love of ours.

I've never experienced
anything like it before."

"You're saying it,"
he responds, casually.
"So why do I have to?"

"Because I want completion.
The feeling of eternity."

"You women are all alike.
You want to take possession,
to make me your slave.
Well, you'll never
own me —
not in a million years."

"No.
I only want you in me
like a small, small tree.
I would know
I have you always,
especially when our lovemaking
is consummated,
and you turn away
and leave."

"Ravenous woman!
You howled with pleasure.
But that's not enough.
You want to devour me
until I'm lodged
inside your body."

"Not so! Not devoured!
Alive inside me instead.
Offer me the warmth
of your open heart,
scream out your love
until the heavens
beam with delight."

"I can't, I won't," he says
in agitation.
"Try!" I say.
"Be there! Be vulnerable!
Open your heart.
Let me in.
I would hold your Self
like a hummingbird,
so gently, so tenderly.
Let me in,
Let me in."

He turns away.
I tell him sadly:
"Pay heed, my love.
I want more, more,
and more —
a warm, tender,
heavenly love —
a love filled with God's truth."

Our wholeness cannot happen
if we are split apart.

We might as well admit:
"We can't —
because —
we won't love You,

God."

23

The Promised Land

I had made a contract to work with an Israeli professional dance company for two months. With the company's well-trained dancers, I had the opportunity to explore the concepts I evolved in America.

I watched my choreographed movements through their bodies, bodies that seemed freer than American dancers' bodies. I found myself pleased with what I had devised over the many years I had been exploring movement based on Bioenergetic concepts. I realized that acceptance by the American dance world would surely remain difficult, but I felt I could return to the American scene with greater confidence. My experimentation seemed not so radical in Israel as it had been in New York City, and once again I received applause after every teaching experience.

I enjoyed the cultural differences, the semitropical climate, the biblical history of the country—particularly that of Jerusalem, to which I traveled twice a week to teach. Socially there was a familiar European quality in the atmosphere, enhanced by my knowledge of French and German, the two fundamental languages spoken there besides English. I felt at home.

I had walked away from Ivan, my stocky lover, released from pain. But the longing for a male connection kept him in my thoughts. I sat in outdoor cafes, thinking nostalgically of our past.

Suddenly, one day, as though dropped from the heavens, a handsome man stood before my table. He bowed graciously, introduced himself, and asked to join me. I was reluctant to leave my dreamy reminiscences, but consented. He explained that his name was Gerard and that he was a medical doctor in the hospital at which I had been given a flu shot. He had noticed me in the waiting room and had followed me for several days. He had wanted to approach me before, but had been afraid. Since I had looked so forlorn, he now mustered the courage to introduce himself to me.

I was astonished by his candor, his attraction to me, his charm. I was reluctant to believe he was not a heavenly angel sent as a reward for the new strength I had found to walk away from Ivan. He was without a mate, he was my age and he was overwhelmed by my beauty, he said. I pinched myself to see if I was indeed awake.

He asked if he could accompany me to my room and if I would consent to see him the next evening for dinner. I nodded foggily. After his departure that evening, I looked up at the night sky. The stars blinked and blinked as they had done when I was a child. I went to bed, urging time to move speedily to hasten our appointed rendezvous.

We met. As we spoke — in English, for everyone in Israel speaks English—he intimated that as soon as he had seen me, he had thought of marrying me. I was dumbfounded by his ardent desire, his conviction that I was the right mate for him. Again I attributed this gift of being wanted by a man, a man who was established in the world, a man who thought I was beautiful, to bountiful deities. They had finally given me recognition for my goodness.

I became ungrounded, and I obsessed over this mystical "approval." Without knowing much more about the doctor, I impulsively moved into his apartment. He was handsome; he had come to Israel with his parents after the Russian occupation of his country; he longed for freedom from tyranny. He wanted a family, but most of all he wanted a beautiful, interesting woman for his mate.

His apartment was small but cozy. It surpassed by far the furnished room in which I had been closeted since my arrival in Israel. He showed me his neighborhood and introduced me to his friends. On the weekends we drove to other parts of the country—such as the Sea of Galilee, which fascinated me, always sending a mysterious chill up my spine, a feeling as if I had been there before.

He supported my culinary efforts and, in time, I became an excellent cook. He was interested in my activities, my thoughts, my feelings. He would return in the late afternoon from the hospital and ask me how my day had passed. No one had ever shown such concern. Again I felt I was living on manna from heaven.

Our sexual connection was problematic, though I was patient with the frequency of his premature ejaculations, because I thought we were connecting from our hearts.

We spoke of marriage and decided I should first return to America to take care of my affairs. I agreed, eager to get the sanction of my guru in this monumental matter.

After two months of living with the doctor-lover, I returned to America. I asked Dr. Warner about the doctor's sexual difficulties. He shrugged the matter aside and suggested I give him time. With this sanction tucked neatly into my psyche and with my guru's willingness to let go of me, I left America. I was ready to live in a new country, with a new man, and to teach dance to a professional dance company.

When I returned to Israel, the apartment was filled with flowers. He had waited impatiently for my return, he had bought things to make me more comfortable, I had brought gifts for him from America, the land of plenty. He adored me. I received his adoration.

He was a sensitive, intellectual man, with a gentility unfamiliar to me, and his kindness brought out my true nature. I had striven for emotional freedom most of my life, through movement and as a human being. I was known and appreciated for such energy. The more gentle he became, the more I emerged as my rambunctious, expressive self — at least at the beginning of our relationship.

His mode of expression, in contrast to mine, was restricted and contained. As he became acquainted with my moving, expressive body, he became increasingly critical of its freedom. I had the disquieting impression I was again being put into a container and pushed down into a well. He suggested I use fewer body gestures when I spoke, that I sit with my legs pressed tightly together, with the hem of my dress pulled well below my knees. He also suggested I be more reserved with other male acquaintances. It was all too reminiscent of my parents' home.

I thought he was joking until, late one evening after a social affair, I saw my supposed "gentleman" inebriated from large amounts of brandy, smoking a foul-smelling cigar, and accusing me of inappropriate behavior with the host of the party. The host of the party, unknown to me, was a notorious womanizer, despite his marriage. I was astounded by the false accusation. I did not sleep for the rest of the night.

In the morning, Gerard awakened and greeted me with his usual kind and loving demeanor. The chaotic evening was gone from his mind, but I was left with the emotional debris. When I attempted to speak to him about the night before, he gave me gifts. I was won over temporarily, but the incident, aggravated by our continuingly inadequate sex, began to gnaw at me incessantly.

In time, though, the warmth between us returned as he attended to me — devotedly, sensitively, caringly. I lost myself in the relationship once again as I chattered noisily about my ideas, what parts of the country I wanted to see, and the dance gossip of the company I was teaching. He participated in these discussions with humor and interest. At one point, however, I noticed him withdraw abruptly after I related a conversation I had had with a male student dancer in a cafe. He began to question me in a skillful, suspicious manner about the appearance of the dancer, his age, and the topic of our conversation; I noticed he wanted minute descriptions of our interaction. When I blithely skipped to another topic, he returned aggressively to his original questioning mode, until I became exasperated and left the room.

My unwillingness to comply with his subtle grilling must have fueled his paranoia, and for several weeks after, he became totally withdrawn, a state I began referring to as his "deep freeze."

At such times, I occupied myself creatively by concocting original recipes and serving the food to a silent, distant partner. Three weeks became his average "deep-freeze" time period, after which he would emerge from the self-inflicted incarceration and seduce me once again with his charm, his devotion, and his gifts. Meanwhile, I had acquired a new addiction: being cared for and paid attention to.

Our sexual encounters became increasingly farcical due to his impotence. After each sexual fiasco, though, his Olympian caring would again ensnare me.

The culmination of our subliminal conflict occurred at the time of meeting his parents. It was a significant event for him because he had never before introduced a woman to them, and since we were considering marriage, the meeting was necessary and appropriate.

We prepared happily for the party and included our friends in the important occasion. After my introduction to his family, we were scheduled to fly to Eilat, a desert in the south of Israel.

We were unduly excited, and when the day finally came, I waited nervously for the parents' arrival. He assured me that they would love me, and I hoped I might gain better parents than my own had been. Everyone was merrily drinking and partaking of my gourmet repast. It was beyond the anticipated time of their coming when I realized I had almost forgotten the real reason for the occasion. Just then, they arrived.

I remember sitting on a chair in view of the open door. The guests were involved with one another, scattered around the room. At that moment I had taken a seat to rest my legs. As I bent over to disengage my feet from my shoes, two elderly people glided noiselessly into the room, walked deliberately toward me, gesticulated wildly into my face, made a military about-face, and bolted out the door.

I remember trying to put my feet into my shoes, attempting to stand up while partially unshod, and extending my arm to greet the two invaders. What I experienced was the venomous after-draft coming toward me from their abrupt exit. The room fell silent; the party was over. I was stunned.

I looked for Gerard. He appeared with our suitcases and insisted I immediately get ready to leave, pushing me into his car for our drive to the airport. He told me that someone would be coming the next day to take care of the cleaning. He spoke little, commenting on the success of the party. When I asked about the behavior of his parents, he changed the subject. An hour later, we were in a desert hotel.

Our trip to the desert summed up our life together. I was fascinated by the terrain. I had never before been to a desert and was overcome by the beauty of the sunsets, the mystery of the desolate landscape, the phenomenon of the Red Sea.

Gerard did not acknowledge my appreciation because he had sunk into another "deep freeze" state. I had to fend for myself. I dared not converse with others because of his paranoid tendencies. We did not make love. He would not discuss the meeting with his parents. I could not cook because we were in a hotel. I became rambunctiously miserable and suggested we leave. He complied, remaining silent the entire trip home.

The looming of the 1967 Six Days' War soon thereafter sent me home to America, with renewed determination to understand the patterns that seemed to control my life and thwart my being.

24

Two Phallic Men, Two Passive Men

My life —
a whirlwind of confusion:
two phallic men,
two passive men.
Neither served my nature.

My nature —
What is that?
"Who are you, Anneliese?"

"Who are you, really?"

I wanted a male
who was kind and loving,
sexual as well as
brilliant.
Sean was sexual,
but very lost;
Ivan — sexual, but
confused.

Michael and Gerard:
Oh, so passive —
weakened by their mothers —
the fathers whom they emulated
so fearful, disempowered.

Sean and Ivan:
mother-dominated.
Their brutal fathers
conferred power
on their psyches.
Power misperceived by me
as strength,
until I recognized their cruelty.
Cruelty like my papa's.

"What am I looking for?
Why always these aborted
relationships?
What am I doing
to attract such men?"
They are who they are.
The choices are mine.

My background
was dysfunctional.
That's the truth.
But there are other reasons
why relationships abort.
You, my "I," are stronger
than before;
but
what ails you still?

I am unbalanced.
My male is ineffectual.
The weakness comes
from my papa.
I attract what is familiar.
It is an unconscious seeking.
Magnetized,
these men and I
find each other.

Balance is what I long for.
Men must be seen
in other ways . . . .

But how?

25

The Next Phase

A fter I returned to New York, my guru, Dr. Roger Warner, now booking patients months in advance, got in touch with me. Because of the extensive amount of Bioenergetic work I had done and my background in body training and awareness, he wanted to send patients to me for additional body work. This put me into the position of adjunct to him and the therapy he was doing with patients. I therefore began participating actively in the psychological world, which eventually started me on the path to a new career. This was very opportune, since I had become tired of my impoverished existence as a dancer. I realized I was ready for a radical change.

I embarked enthusiastically upon the new field, utilizing my dance background along with Bioenergetic tools. I finally received professional sanction for my ideas, contrary to the hostile reception they formerly received in the dance field.

It seemed that my world was becoming clearer, as in the happy ending of a fairy tale. I was on my way to achieving an "I" state of consciousness: I had become assertive, psychologically clearer, economically solvent, connected to a profession in which I was respected.

Despite these accomplishments, however, I remained unresolved about a mate. I did not yet dare totally discard the male imagery of my guru, particularly since I was now dealing with the varied and complicated behavior of others' psyches, and my guru's aura of self-confidence solved any deficiency in my own male energy.

As for my personal therapy with Dr. Warner, because of his busy schedule, he suggested I work with his colleague. I accepted the change because I knew I would more readily be able to explore the sticky, unclear transference to my guru with another therapist.

I also looked at my hatred and anger toward men. The purging of such feelings gave me energetic relief, but I felt that the relief was short-lived. No matter how much I purged myself of these feelings, they needed to be addressed repeatedly.

I decided to remain alone, no longer wishing to become involved in another entangled, messy alliance with a man until I felt clearer not only about who I was, but why I had chosen the men of the past.

All the while I asked, "Who am I, God? Who am I, really?" My underlying question remained: "Why do my relationships abort? What role do I play in them? Who am I, as a woman?"

I watched others' relationships with great curiosity, while I concentrated on my place in the world, exploring with great diligence the male-female issue as well as other aspects of myself.

I wandered into many paths, looking, searching, never fully clear about my own path, but nevertheless restlessly searching. I was propelled in new directions by my soul's yearning to be incorporated into a meaningful Self. I was ready to embrace the next domain of myself.

This fact became particularly clear when I had the following dream:

> Two male astronauts were scheduled to be sent into the atmosphere in a spaceship. They were terrified because the astronauts in the previous expedition had not returned. The two astronauts were pale with fear. One of them had difficulty standing on his feet. The other was braver. When take-off time was announced, I supported the more fearful one as he stumbled on his way to the spacecraft. He entered it, smiling weakly at me.

PART THREE

The "I AM"

*"Each soul and spirit, prior to entering into
this world, consists of a male and female
united into one being.
" . . . forming as it were the right and left of
one individual."*

— Christian D. Ginsburg

26

The Keys to the Self

In Israel, before I had met Gerard, on the eve of the celebration of the birth of Jesus, in the city of Bethlehem, I looked at the night sky; the stars blinked vibrantly. My heart swelled with familiar feelings: feelings of longing, of homesickness, of wishing to be touched by something bigger than what I had known. My tears began to flow, with an indescribable ecstasy. They became anguished tears, as I identified the feeling of wanting to go home. I wanted to go home, back to my real home: to the spheres from which I had originally come.

I realized then that I belonged somewhere else, that Earth was not my true home. The Earth experience was merely a transition in time, giving me valuable lessons.

The tears continued to flow strongly and steadily, until I was exhausted. I sat under the stars, knowing that my consciousness had been changed. My heart had opened. The seams were not so tightly knit. A sweet, tender smile of gentleness emerged. I perceived it as a secret between God and me. A quietude grew inside me, which has been there ever since, even though the constant turbulent unraveling of my psyche continues alongside.

The sweet gentle feelings of that night made my heart roar for more. My heart drove me to search beyond the therapeutic process, to other processes that enabled me to recapture such feelings. I learned also that the need to satisfy those feelings did not always have the same intensity, because often they became eclipsed by the vicissitudes of life. At other times, however, the need screamed forth with its original force, setting me into motion to requite the longing. At such times I became obsessed with ridding myself of the chattering, cacophonous voices of the psyche, with drowning out the doubts and fears that contended with the sweet, gentle voices discovered in Bethlehem.

There was seldom time to capture that sweetness, to coax it back into my system. So I looked for help in America. I found a woman who taught in a church, with whom I sat in meditation and with whom I was able to capture "it" again.

"It" was like trying to catch a firefly. When the insect was finally caught in my hand and I opened my hand enough to see the light, the firefly would fly away, away from my anxious grasp. I would then sit in utter frustration, wondering how I could have held onto it, if I should leave life and become a nun, dedicating myself to the search for God.

The teacher in the church said that I must learn to focus inwardly so completely that I would be able to reach God even in such a bedlam environment as a Middle Eastern marketplace.

For a time, I hurried during my lunch break to sit at the feet of this woman, who would help me renew my experience of that longed-for Bethlehem sweetness. I would return to work, resentful of the circumscribed nature of my life. I was faced with learning to deal with life, yet staying in touch with the Bethlehem feelings. I juggled all the time, becoming aware that if the Earth reality was not attended to, chaos would manifest. On the other hand, if I did not seek my Bethlehem feelings, I would be left in an empty, unfulfilled existence.

I traveled to India, Ceylon, Mexico in pursuit of an enlightened being who would direct me, guide me, gaze on my countenance and tell me I was divine. I received that attention from almost all of them. I finally realized that I had been traveling long distances and at great expense to be told I was like the rest of humanity. I had connected to this need, and like many others, got caught in the chase for approval from the enlightened one.

A sage might or might not, during a morning or afternoon meeting with his disciples, deign to give a devotee personal attention or a private audience. Congregated searchers sat in the hot sun and sand, waiting expectantly as the anointed one walked among his followers, bestowing holy ash on the selected few. Holy ash was an elixir substance produced from the atmosphere with a twist of the hand. The procedure reminded me of the biblical reference to manna emerging from the heavens, feeding the Hebrews after their exodus from Egypt.

I was one of those selected by the sage, not only to witness the production of the elixir substance, but to receive it. The holy one, as he was referred to, poured the grey substance into the palm of my hand and instructed me to eat it. When I did so, I became intoxicated with the smell and taste of the ash and folded the rest of it into a tissue. Many years have passed since the experience, but I can attest to the fact that the tissue containing the elixir is still in my possession, and supply is never depleted by use. Somehow it remains magically replenished.

After I received this great honor, the rest of the seekers congregated around me, dabbing their fingers into the substance, touching my garments, hoping indirectly to imbibe some of the sage's divine vibration. I remember how exalted I felt by the attention of the holy one, yet how uncomfortable I became by the desperate behavior of the followers. I wondered if I too would grovel like them for his attention; whether I would become obsessed by the need for his sanction of my divinity; whether, like most of his followers, I would make pilgrimage upon pilgrimage to this particular place in India, enduring the difficult climate and the horrendous living conditions, participating in their obsessive, manic ways. I wondered, on the last day of my stay in India, as I sat in the hot sun and the sand, waiting for the avatar, the anointed one, to arrive, if this was truly my path to God.

When I returned to America and asked this question of the teacher in the church, she looked at me quietly and suggested that the trips I had taken in search of an avatar to give me enlightenment might not be the right course of action for me. After considerable hesitation, she told me I might need to search for God directly within.

Her words put me into conflict. She was telling me to find my own way, which, at that time, was too frightening, since it made me feel once again my separateness from others. But I was also astute enough to understand that pursuing another "guru," whether he be a psychological one or a spiritual one, had become an outmoded pattern for me. I therefore ceased my travels to find sages in foreign lands and looked for answers within.

I discovered the metaphysical realm of religion. I learned that I was of the substance of God and that I, therefore, possessed the attributes of God. I liked this idea; it gave me the hope and faith that I was more than the prototype of my parents' images.

On Sundays I began attending the meetings of a metaphysical group. I traveled two hours to arrive at the meeting hall; there was an enlightened sermon, followed by announcements and singing, but I waited impatiently for the lights to dim for a ten-minute meditation, in which the leader of the group invited the participants to "go within."

I had traveled two hours for this moment — for a ten-minute connection to my "within." That "within" connection reminded me of the Bethlehem feeling. I screamed inwardly with indignation when the lights were turned on and a donation basket was shoved into my lap. I needed more time to "go within." Did they not know that my Bethlehem feeling was there, and that I was desperate to reach it?

At the beginning of this new adventure I would leave the meetings satisfied. But eventually my frustration became overwhelming. I looked at the practicing metaphysicians and their readied, radiant smiles. I wondered how they handled their negative thoughts, their negative backgrounds, their frustrations in life. In observing their bodies Bioenergetically, I noticed how little they were in contact with themselves. I questioned if, by adhering to this philosophy, I would again be splitting off from my psyche.

It had not yet occurred to me that the process of "going within" might not necessitate the sanction of a leader, a guru, an avatar, a teacher. It had not occurred to me that I could "go within" on my own. Eventually I left that movement too, continuing my search for a way to connect the psychological with the "within."

As one always does, I found that place on my doorstep. My new therapist, Dr. Phillip Reed, had separated from my guru and allied himself with a woman who was a medium. He too was looking for a more holistic approach to the psyche. The medium, a foreign-born, attractive woman named Inge, sat in front of followers in a trance, channeling an otherworld entity to speak through her.

I listened to its messages. I realized that concepts such as reincarnation, karma, taking responsibility for one's actions, functioning from inner truth were advocated. I attended the groups enthusiastically, hopeful that answers about my true self would be forthcoming, that my Bethlehem feeling would be activated.

My relationship to all men was an issue immediately under scrutiny. Inge, Dr. Reed, and the group insisted I inform my guru, Dr. Warner, of my connection to them. I was reluctant, but I did, telling him in a letter that I wanted to deal more spiritually with my psyche and would no longer be able to assist him in his workshops. No answer came. I continued my therapeutic process with them.

It was a rigorous experience. Their method of direct confrontation terrified me; my defenses became so heightened that my impulse was to run away from contact with the group activities. I felt as though I were repeatedly pushed against a stone wall and pummeled by rocks until I would either capitulate or die. It felt like a Nazi inquisition. My need for isolation was understood by them to originate from fear of people, which was interpreted as a defense against my rage and hatred of people. Rage, hatred, and fear of people were not justifiable feelings, no matter what injustices had been suffered. Immediate recantation was required or else more accusations, more stoning would result.

I learned I was a demanding woman with men, either castrating them or choosing to be victimized by them. I tried to tell them that I agreed with many of their analyses, but that my innate rhythm needed consideration. My innate rhythm, I tried to convey to them, could be grasped through the lines from Virginia Woolf: "I want to love and be loved, and time to unfold my possessions." This need of mine was dismissed as a defensive avoidance.

It was mandatory to attend Inge's monthly lectures. I began unconsciously rejecting every word that came from her mouth, but I denied my reaction. I sat at the meetings, ill at ease, making myself impervious to her and the rest of the attendees. I was baffled that the followers seemed genuinely awestruck as the oracle spoke, some holding their hands in her direction to imbibe her miraculous energy. Dr. Reed sat by her side, entranced, adoring, certain he had found the answers not only to a new psychology, but to life itself.

I was again the outsider; I did not belong. My psychological mother and father, from whom I was getting guidance, were synchronous with each other and with their world, their followers. Their followers were synchronous with them. As always I was left out, out in the cold.

"What is wrong with me?" was my private, agonized thought. "I must be demented. I'm always critical, always at odds with what is going on. I invariably find myself in this position. They cannot all be wrong. I don't belong anywhere. I want to die."

I sank backward, backward into my old "not I" state. They noticed my withdrawal. They shunned me. Then came another confrontation. I blurted out to them that I felt that Inge, the medium, was evil. They were stunned. I was a traitor and they treated me like Judas Iscariot.

I was riddled with guilt for my feelings, feelings that had come out of my mouth without my control. I had no idea who was speaking when I uttered those blasphemous words.

I felt crazed, but unlike Judas, I did not hang myself. Instead, I thrashed about, solitary in my miserable dilemma. Once again the world was a black, inky ocean of despair into which I had fallen and in which I trod water frantically, looking for the direction of survival.

Although present in body, I had emotionally removed myself from their midst because of my conviction that I was right. As a result, Dr. Reed and Inge excommunicated me officially and took away the clients with whom we had worked mutually. Their castigation created a deep hole in my finances, necessitating my starting anew.

I had not shared this with anyone, keeping the tension bottled up inside me. I was becoming physically ill. No longer able to restrain myself, I told a professional person of my difficult situation. To my astonishment, he agreed with my assessment of the organization and the medium. I trusted his judgment because he had been intimately connected to all concerned: Dr. Reed, the medium and the organization.

His confirmation of my intuitive assessment relieved me considerably. I regained confidence that my perceptions were not crazy.

I was adamant about no longer fooling myself and not putting myself into a victim position. I questioned myself thoroughly about a woman like Inge, who easily could represent my authoritarian mamma.

I was convinced there was another reality, however, that needed probing. Since I was unable to identify this reality, I consulted a psychic, a total stranger, who informed me that in a past life I had been controlled by a medium, who had used me to serve the questionable purposes of a community. I heard this reading, but could not quite accept that my perceptions that she was evil were valid. There were too many pieces that needed to be uncovered before the puzzling matter could be validated. In the meantime, I tucked it away in my unconscious.

I was soothed by the professional person's affirmation of my intuition. I was also appeased by the psychic's reading. Even though I had been affirmed, I did not probe further into the meaning of the experience, until later in my psychological unraveling. Instead, I wallowed masochistically in the consciousness that I was once again the odd kid on the block. I realized vaguely that I derived a certain amount of pleasure from my outcast state, taking from it the sense of "specialness." But I let go of the matter as I attended to the reality of reconstructing my practice.

My wounds healed in time, and my practice grew more solvent. I also gained satisfaction, five years later, when a few members of the organization got in touch with me and apologized for their former cruelty. They too had been excommunicated by the authorities for daring to question their credo. They had been labeled fascists, psychopaths, and other reprehensible names. They were now floundering, as I had done, looking for a truer anchor for their lives. I was sympathetic to their plight, but avoided further contact.

I dreamed a memorable dream about my own plight. One night, before retiring, I programmed my unconscious mind to give me the answer to my outcast feelings, which reminded me of being a leper no one wanted to approach. I was aware that groups of people terrified me; much as I wanted a social as well as a professional connection to people, I was unsuccessful at achieving one. When I asked my unconscious mind what I should do about belonging, I received the following dream:

> I saw an older woman holding an infant. The infant put her hands
> on each of the woman's breasts. She then placed the nipples of
> the breasts into the woman's mouth.

I interpreted the dream to mean that I must nurture myself and live my life from my own incentives. I finally understood that I was on my own path, persevering on my path. I began to understand that my attempts to follow others' paths were disastrous for me, were against my destiny.

The dream had a powerful effect on me. I decided to continue my education. I enrolled in a doctoral program in psychology. Since I needed an established Bioenergetic psychiatrist to serve on my doctoral committee, I approached my former guru, Dr. Warner. We had had no contact for a number of years.

He welcomed me with open arms and made himself immediately available for the project. He was proud of my latest endeavor, and we quickly reestablished our connection, synchronizing our creative efforts, always the most dynamic aspect of our relationship.

I looked at him with amusement, because it was clear that his primary interest in me involved the retrieval of one of his lost sheep. I sensed his certitude that all who had left the fold would eventually return to his shepherding. Should they not, like his former colleague Dr. Reed, they remained lost sheep.

He did not believe in the concepts I had been working with in the other group. But since we were both good diplomats, we avoided any reference to such topics. After I obtained my degree, I saw him only infrequently. But I always remained affected by his charismatic energy. I felt grateful for the work we had done together, and I retained the male imagery I had imbibed from him. This male energy pertained mostly to Bioenergetic tools. My personal male energy remained, unfortunately, my father's.

I was a workaholic, abstaining from personal contact with men because I was fearful of being rejected or rejecting them — fearful of falling into unwanted, familiar patterns. I concentrated on my work and the people in my practice, at the same time unraveling my psyche, trying to get resolution regarding my real identity.

I worked with others' psyches, becoming more and more aware of the massive *undoing* a clear state of mind required. I saw both how complicated and how necessary it is to eradicate one's parents' imprints in order to touch upon one's real self. I kept wondering, "Where is the intrinsic self? How does one realize it?"

I sat by myself meditatively one day and asked:

> Self,
> the golden glimmer,
> the connectedness
> that brings peace and joy
> to the system.
> The undivided, harmonious,
> sweet, existing place
> in the psyche.
>
> Where do you reside?
> What must I do to pull
> you out of your hiding place?
> Can you not see that I have
> traveled halfway round the
> globe in search of you?

I know what it means to feel my body,
to feel my senses as they respond to
life,
to feel pain, joy, anguish, ecstasy.
I have worked many years to have
such feelings,
but —
there is more.

I know there is more;
for, if not,
my being would rest
and be at peace.
I exist, but my existence
is bittersweet.

I have experienced the more.
My soul has bestowed this gift
upon me
when it was least expected.

What must I do to
gain it eternally?

I witnessed the vast, dark, blue sky and saw myself arriving among the stars, my favorite habitat since childhood. I chose one and explored it. I saw unrecognizable shapes around me. One of the shapes evolved into a human form, an ancient man with white hair and a long white beard. He invited me to sit at a large table and to ask my question again. On doing so, I heard a voice within me say:

"Go within — within, within, further within. Ferret out the deepest places, no matter how ugly, how sinful, how divine, how beautiful. Ferret them out and look at them. The Self is a precious gem, an

extension of God. Its need for life's experiences has obscured its perfection.

"Ferret out the darkest places and they will give you the keys to your Self. Know them so you can appreciate, restrain, purify, embellish that essence which is You. Accept this information and unashamedly recognize who you are and who you have been. Look at your male energy. Ask again and again why your relationships were unsatisfactory. Realize that you are in the center of every experience: directing, commanding, reacting, acting.

"No matter how abused you were in your household, you were still in the center of the matter. You chose a stance: pain, victimization, retreat. Why one and not another? Your behavior comes from you, derived from your experiences in this life and other lives."

27

Karma, Reincarnation

I had little difficulty accepting that our lives are involved with karma, the spiritual law of cause and effect, and that one's destiny is determined by what one has sown in previous lives.

I recalled when I was eleven, trying to cope with my life at home: either to commit suicide or go insane. I decided to stay in reality, feeling that whatever karma I had undertaken in this life needed to be dealt with rather than postponed to another life.

It baffles me to this day how I knew about karma and reincarnation. I had made the choice at such an early age not to avoid my destiny, but to face it.

I therefore became an agent for my soul, as we all are. I knew intuitively that when we tune in and listen, there is no greater guidance. I said out loud to others in my childlike way, "If I have to endure in another life what I have had to endure in this one, I'd rather go through whatever trials are in store for me now than avoid them and postpone them for another life." I did not know then the Sanskrit word *samskara*, which refers to the repetitive pattern of behavior lodged in the unconscious from past reactions to difficult karma.

In my journey to the heavens I was advised by my inner voices that I was in the center of my action. I began to understand that reincarnation and karma beget one another. From listening to my higher self, I was finally willing to accept that fact and motivated to undo my psychic distortions.

I believe that were we to be educated in the idea that our lives are manifold, manifesting periodically in a physical body and directed by our karma, we might wish to make our journey to Earth not only more conscious, but more significant. Rectification, redemption, and resurrection could be concepts we live from—concepts that strengthen us to move on our path with greater conviction about our life on Earth.

Is it not the purpose of one's life to resurrect oneself to a closer union with the intrinsic Self, arriving finally at God-consciousness? In order to arrive at a higher consciousness, I realized I must "go within," giving myself the keys to the Self.

28

From My Self to Myself

I speak to you, child.
You refuse to hear.
Has My voice become
that of a parent?

I am not their voices.
I am the voice of your soul.
Won't you listen?

I can answer your questions.
I have an overview,
energized by God's
heavenly wisdom.

Let go of your defenses.
Let me in.
We have been connected,
FOREVER.

You listen a little —
only when you are desperate.

You do not feel worthy
of My Presence.

Separate me from them:
I am your heavenly Self.
Let me guide you.
Tune in.
Know —
You and I are
ONE.

Fuse with Me.
You want this.
It is a test.
Let go of your
"little will."
Let go.
FAITH IS IN QUESTION.

Come, child,
RISK!

Give me —

YOU!

29

Reflections of Our Parents

*D*o *You mean that not all of our lives are totally distorted and unbalanced? Do You mean that I might have had lives of fulfillment, perhaps a life in which I was my beautiful, lyrical female self and a strong pioneering male self? Is it possible that I accumulated good qualities from other lives, qualities nestled in obscure niches of my psyche, whispering the energy of truth alongside the distorted energy of my present female self and the weak male self? Are these niches the source of my talent as a dancer? Are they also the hiding place of the strong, healthy male within me, of whom I have had only fleeting glimpses — with whom I am barely acquainted?*

Are you saying that each life calls forth aspects of the psyche needing to be purged of sin and guilt, aspects not dealt with in other lives, and in the present life emerging as dominant patterns to be rectified? If that is the case, then is it not my task in this lifetime to purify my female energy, strengthen my male energy, and bring balance between the two?

The room became dark . . . or was it my consciousness?
I felt I was falling backward into blackness. The fall
was slow, unbearably slow, as in a dream state. I was
aware only of the shift in my balance.

I shook my head to regain another reality, but nothing —
nothing deterred that backward fall into space. I
continued to fall until I was there.
Where?
There!

Another time, another world, another me.
Is this when it began —
the unbalance of my female and male energies?

Perhaps!
Oh, God!
What are you doing to mc?

The answer that came was:

> *Man —— fence.*
> *The fence cannot be*
> *jumped over.*
> *It has no gate.*

> *I ask myself*
> *"Why is the fence*
> *a barrier ——*
> *to the man?"*

> *The answer —*
> *I have put it there.*
> *I put it there because*
> *the man ——*
> *is not accessible to me.*

I put it there
because my mother
does not want me to
—— have a man.

She is the only one
worthy of having a man.
If I do not heed her
unspoken command,
—— I will be punished.

Mother is the beauty
of the village.
No one is permitted to
compete with her.

How would I feel if
the fence were taken down?

I answer:
I would devour the
man's penis.
I would slowly eat his flesh
like a praying mantis.
I would then have him
inside me.
I would nourish him
as I wish to be nourished.

He would be my male!

I cannot have a male of my own
because of the queen.
Only she can have her own man.

If the man lives inside my body,
No one will know I have an
attachment to a male.

If I had my own male,
I would get torn
limb —— from —— limb.

Such is the regulation
of the tribe, wherein a man
is a captured slave.

I am always —— lonely.
I can never love a man,
because the queen assigns
first one —— then —— another
to me.

My heart is always broken.
My attachments are always
—— broken.
Attachment
seems a natural way to live.

It cannot be for me,
nor the other women
of the tribe.

Once, one of the women
in the tribe
fell in love with a slave.
Their love was discovered
—— they were killed!

Their death was brutal and terrible.
Such is the way of our queen.

She is good in many ways,
but —
she will have no one as strong as she
— nor with the same
privileges.

I pounce upon men for sex.
That is the way of the tribe.
I use them —
am dispassionate toward them.

The men hate us —
we women behave inhumanly.
If only I could tell them,
"I cannot help myself.
I am too frightened to
oppose the queen!"

I now want desperately to
have a male for myself.
I need to experience loving
a male and being
loved by him.

One day —
I too fall in love.
I go to the queen,
tell her I want my lover
for my husband.
She pretends to consent.

A child grows within me.
When it is large in my womb,
her henchmen come to my
quarters in the night —
dislodge it.
—— I bleed to —— death.

It is not that I do not
want a man or his energy
in me.
I am afraid —
not to follow the tribal ways,
for fear of a horrible
—— death ——

Is not the soul male and female?
I cannot return to the heavens
unless this is remedied.

This is the fence —— I have
—— erected —— a fence of
protection,
a fence against being bludgeoned
—— to death ——
because —
I want to love a man.

The human shape is a ghost
made of distraction and pain.
Sometimes pure light, sometimes cruel,
trying wildly to open,
this image tightly held within itself.

—Rumi

30

Resurrection

I wrote this poem after experiencing that first "memory":

> The coward in me lurks deep inside.
> It waits for me to be weakened,
> by the shouts, the boos, the
> enraged mob.
>
> It speaks to me, its victim:
> "Fool, give up!
> They will murder you.
> Slink away into oblivion.
> If you do it my way,
> you'll not be hurt.
> You can live your life,
> untortured.
>
> "They will crucify you.
> They will hang you from the
> rafters.
> They will burn you at the stake,
> as they burned so many others.

"Now is the time to save yourself.
Be of them, the adjusted people.
Don't wait for God.
He forsook you before.
I, your coward, have
kept you alive.

"Your cowardice is the voice
of your
redemption."

I tell my coward:
"Yes, you have protected me
from the pain of torture.
Yet my cowardice has tortured
me in ways that have no language.
If life means living cowardly,

"then,
I will listen only to my
inner voice,
which speaks to me of
resurrection.

"There is no room for your
shrieking.
I want no more of your lies.
I will purge myself of the
horror of earlier existences,

"when
torture
made me cower.

"Now,
I will never let you take me over.
I will choose death,
instead.

"God!
Give me the courage to
love truth more.
Give me the strength to
rectify my misdeeds,
to fight for a balanced nature.

"Let my light finally
join with

Yours."

31

The Male Within

Eagerly, now, yet still fearfully, I went deep, deep, back into the long-buried memories. I felt myself, suddenly, as a warrior in search of my destiny, a warrior intent on changing my destiny, a warrior searching to complete my destiny. I went back again, deep within myself. Beyond my self, to my Self.

The fifteenth century, a handsome young man, idealistic, exuberant about what he was teaching, beloved by his students. His ideas were exciting but controversial. The elders in the school in which he was employed shook their heads, smiling at him ingratiatingly, thinking his radical mind was a product of his youth. They thought that in time, life and experience would temper his imaginative, fertile brain. He was the darling of the community; the elders invited him to every event, where he was fawned on by all. At one of these fetes, he met a young, beautiful woman, the daughter of one of the elders. He fell hopelessly in love and married her soon after. They celebrated their wedding for a week.

As the years passed, the elders felt that his influence on the minds of the young students was becoming problematic, as the students began to rebel against the elders' rigid beliefs. They shunned the elders' classes and flocked instead to the young man's, cheering his ideas. The elders felt humiliated and became furious.

At first, the young man was admonished gently by the elders, urged to revert to a less individualistic way of teaching — at least, one which would not depart so radically from theirs. He listened to them respectfully, but could not compromise himself. His young wife, who was appealed to by her father, also urged her husband to return to a more conventional approach to his work so they could continue their peaceful, harmonious, and luxurious life. He heard her pleas, but he could not do it. Instead, he taught more fervently in his way than ever; the students continued to flock to his classes and laud his ideas.

The elders admonished him again. This time they uttered ominous warnings about his future if he did not change his methods of teaching. Finally, between the pressure from his wife, who could not withstand the loss of her position in the community, and her father's pressure on both of them, the young man capitulated and repudiated his ideas. He told his students that his ideas were fallacious and not worthy to be considered. He once again resorted to the elders' theories, while his students fell into a gloomy silence.

The students felt baffled and betrayed. They began to ridicule him as a coward. They mocked him during his classes when he stood before them tearfully and begged them to be patient with him; they mocked him when he was seen walking with his wife in the village; they mocked and jeered at him when, out of habit, he came to his classroom and lectured to an empty room. They stood outside the classroom, watching him declaim his theories, perplexed, distraught, slowly losing his sanity.

The young man soon sank into deep despair. He sought compassion from his wife, but she rejected his grief and pushed him away. Eventually, the students ceased to bother about him and returned to the elders' classes. The young man was dismissed from the school as an academic failure. His wife, completely exasperated with him, withdrew her love. He left the school, his home, his wife, and lived in a cave, like a wild beast.

I wandered away from there,
into a cave of misery.
My mind grew crazed

as I tried to understand
what had happened.
But my mind had broken
into many pieces,
as I twittered to myself
incoherently.

I spoke only with the animals.
They looked at me
as I howled like them.
My howls
were of misery and
sorrow.

My mouth was agape.
My finger pointed
at something in the sky.
I asked God,
"What is this about?
Why did You do this to me?"

All at once, my heart stopped.
Such was the sight that
greeted the wife, parents, and elders,
a frozen being,
who had pointed at God —
a crazed face looking
for an answer.

They stared at me,
feeling they had been right
to shun me and my work.
They did not acknowledge
they were using my work

for themselves,
taking credit for its origin.

My wife looked on,
then turned away.
She knew the answer within her,
of how she had broken this
spirit of mine —
to remain
her
father's
daughter.

A dungeon below the ground. A tiny, barred window became visible, the only source of light in the enclosure. A gentle old man with a white beard. He seems to have been in this bondage for many years. His body is emaciated; he has been given just enough food to keep him alive. He saves some crumbs, however, from his meager allotment of food, reaching high to place them on the windowsill. The birds come, pick the crumbs, and eat them. The old man eyes the birds jealously, for they are able to fly away into the sky where no one can thrash them, nor question them over and over again. That has been his fate thus far.

He had been a scientist in the city in which he is imprisoned. He was known to do experiments to improve its welfare. Those who have evil intent toward the city want to pry his secrets from him; when he refuses to divulge them, they imprison him. They torture and starve him, but he will not submit to them. He knows he will never submit to them. His body eventually becomes impervious to the tortures. He hopes they will be over soon, that in time he will fly to the heavens like his beloved birds. Once in heaven he will complain fervently to its inhabitants about man's inhumanity to man.

The guards come to torture him again in order to elicit the desired information. He challenges them to a battle. When they approach him with their torture tools, he stands before them on wobbly legs. In his right hand, he holds the fork with which he has eaten his meager meal. He lifts it above his head as though it were a weapon of destruction and thrusts it toward the enemy. The guards, laughing sinisterly, give him a light shove. He collapses to the ground. He gives a final gasp. On his face is a victorious smile, a smile signifying that he has at last stood up to his tormentors.

Locked in the cellar again.

Three years old, again.

32

Reflections of Mother

I *am in a spacious mansion, attended by slaves, hundreds of years ago.
I am a beautiful woman, the owner of the mansion and the estate to
which it belongs. I see myself pacing back and forth. I am speaking to
a handsome man who stands quietly, patiently before me, listening to my
tirade. At one moment, I rave and rant at him. At another moment I beg
him not to leave me. I give a solemn oath that I will never again be
abusive to him or to the servants on my property, whom I habitually flog
when they have misbehaved or even when they have not.*

*I see myself alternating wildly between pleas of love and threats to
have him flogged to death if he does not obey me. I come closer to him,
desirous of touching him, hoping to entice him to love me despite my
furious outbursts. I run my hands along his body, place my head against
his chest until I feel his breathing. I fuse with it until our breath
becomes one. Eventually he looks down at me, takes my hands in his,
and kisses them. I feel immediately relieved and triumphant. I secretly
rejoice that I have won him over again.*

*He is my husband, a former slave, whom I have grown to need
desperately and to love with an insane passion. I love his gentleness, his
kindness, his integrity, his feelings for other human beings. He once
again takes me to our bedroom, where he tames my passion. He is all
mine and I refuse to share him with anyone.*

Our halcyon days soon end. One day, in my courtyard, I notice him teaching a young male slave. I had seen them together many times, but had curtailed the vengeful fury that arose in me. Suddenly, unable to control myself, I snatch a whip and begin flogging the slave, as if by flogging the innocent being I can rid the earth of his presence. I would have beaten him to death had not my husband, for the first time in our marriage, torn the whip from my hand. He throws it at me and tells the boy to run for safety. He leaves my presence. I grab the whip from the ground and blindly flog the air, destroying whatever is in the way of my insane temper.

When my wrath is spent, I wish to repent. I search for him every-where, but he is not to be found. Obsessed with my need to find him, atone, and win his love again, I eventually leave my mansion. I leave my wealth behind me.

I live my life in relentless guilt. My years of tyranny arise before me as I suffer from the horrible pain of my misdeeds. I yearn for him until, one day, when I can no longer bear the pain, I die with his name on my lips.

There she is — not a pretty sight! My masks have served me well in this life, but she has continued to dance her dance inside me. I have let her out so that you may witness such a monstrosity. If all of you are witnesses, then I need no longer keep her out of view, feeling guilty about her. The reason I had the need to hide her is that I am ashamed of her and repelled by her.

33

Making Peace with My Male

I feel I have been miraculously filled with a sense of purpose. I would like to uncover another male past life to give me a better perspective about my papa's male energy and, of course, my own. I hope and pray that there is a less passive, perhaps even a sadistic male roaming around in my psyche. I want to capture him and that energy so my present male will become clearer.

A man, in the Middle Ages. Tall, strong, and sensitive. In prison, swaggering and boasting about his exploits with women. The other prisoners are hardened murderers and thieves, who would kill him did he not exhibit such bravado.

His childhood, a lonely one. His father is a drunkard who, after his beloved wife's death, blames his son for her death because during her pregnancy she developed a lingering ailment that killed her in childbirth. The father feels righteous in hating and neglecting his son. He soon marries another woman with a daughter. The daughter and son, both of the same age, grow up together. The daughter is favored not only by her mother but by his father. He is beaten regularly for little reason. No matter how much he tries to please his father, he remains an outcast in the family.

Sphinx. Before her death, he had been given this name by his mother, who had loved him and felt his existence on Earth was a miracle and a mystery of God. In order to be accepted by his father, he begins to swagger and boast like him. This elicits some kindness from the father, but most of the time, his father continues either to ignore him or beat him.

Life for Sphinx continues in this way as he grows to be a young man of eighteen. One night the father invites him to drink with him in a neighborhood inn. Sphinx is overjoyed to get his attention. Although he has never drunk liquor before, he tries to match his father's capacity for alcohol by drinking as much, if not more, than he does. He is determined to show his father how much of a comrade he can be.

They arrive home completely intoxicated. The father goes to his wife's bedroom and forces himself upon her sexually. Sphinx, desirous of emulating his father, does the same to his stepsister, who sleeps in a bed next to his. She screams with fright and indignation, waking up her mother and the neighborhood. The neighbors run to Sphinx's house, pull him off his stepsister, and bring him into a clearing in the forest. They tie him to a tree and beat him mercilessly. When the father awakens from his drunken stupor and comes to the scene, he sees Sphinx bloodied and bruised on the tree. Hoping his father will come to his rescue, Sphinx pleads with him silently, but instead, the father turns his back and disappears into his house. Inside he says, "Sphinx deserves the beating."

When the crowd's wrath is spent, they leave. The ropes loosen from Sphinx's body and he falls to the ground, groaning in pain. He drags himself to his room. He packs his clothes, he bathes his wounds by the well. He leaves his home, crawling and stumbling away until he arrives at a shelter in which he hides until he has healed.

To survive, he steals food from a nearby farmer. He steals enough food to keep him alive while he heals. As he regains his strength, he becomes more daring, stealing food in the daytime as well as in the evening. The farmer becomes suspicious and sets a trap. Sphinx's foot gets caught in it. His howls of pain bring the farmer to the scene and Sphinx is taken to prison.

In the prison the inmates watch him, ready to destroy him should he show signs of weakness. He therefore swaggers and boasts, becoming a menacing spectacle, whom they eventually let alone. The authorities also watch the young man defending himself successfully against the dangerous prison rabble. After much consideration they tell him he would make a good soldier. They release him from prison and invite him to join their group—which is housed well, fed well, and paid money for its services.

After exuberant, boastful farewells to the envious prisoners, Sphinx leaves them behind and journeys on horseback with the soldiers to their camp. He keeps boasting and swaggering, well aware that he is being observed and assessed carefully. The soldiers feel they have made a good choice.

Several days later Sphinx goes with them on their daily mission, to learn what his duties will be. He watches the soldiers rounding up captured slaves. The slaves are taken to a river and forced to walk into its depth until they drown. If they resist, they are beheaded. Sphinx watches this deadly mission, becoming pale with horror. The soldiers watch his reactions. Realizing his life is in jeopardy, Sphinx performs for them like a pompous actor. He gestures menacingly at the slaves as they enter the water and, if they are beheaded, he howls with glee. When the soldiers are not looking in his direction, he vomits his food and, panic-stricken, wonders how he can extricate himself from this horrendous situation.

When the sun sets, the river is filled with the slaves' bodies, their decapitated heads and their spilled blood. Sphinx rides silently behind his newly-found comrades, back to the camp. There, they are given gold and each assigned a whore with whom he spends the night.

Sphinx is also assigned a whore, but he spends the night in a restless, terrified sleep from which he awakens repeatedly, shouting to people to save themselves, to run away, to fight. The whore is grateful that her services are not needed and, from time to time, holds his perspiring, agonized body in her arms. In the morning she disappears, but Sphinx knows it is the beginning of another day of horror and massacre. He knows he will no longer remain an observer, but will be compelled to be a participant.

He swaggers and boasts as they give him his assignment. He is ordered to ride along the river's edge and to slash to death whoever resists going into the river. Filled with terror that the soldiers will discover his panic about the mission, Sphinx goes where he is told. He pretends he can handle the assignment.

When he reaches the place where the slaves are being held, he becomes overwhelmed with terror, confusion, and revulsion. Suddenly he begins to shout and scream like a wild man, swinging his sword crazily into the air. From time to time the waving sword bludgeons a slave, but Sphinx is unaware, because his hysteria propels him with a momentum that makes him look demented. Everyone's attention becomes riveted upon him. Totally out of control, he decapitates one of the resistant captives.

Seeing the severed head on the ground, Sphinx gallops away in panic and horror, far beyond where the butchery is taking place. He disappears into the distance, until his shouts and screams are mere echoes in the air. The soldiers in the meantime have lost control over their captives, who flee back to their quarters.

There is no place to which he can flee without being caught. Therefore he returns, dazed, still overwrought and trapped in his hysteria. He is unaware of the havoc he has created. He rides back to the body of the slave he has murdered and stands beside it, transfixed. The soldiers mock him and spit in his face. They return to their barracks without him.

As the sun is setting, Sphinx stands on the same spot, mindless and lost, overcome by his treacherous deed. He looks upon the mutilated body and bangs his head against the ground, hoping to dull his brain. Again and again he bangs his head against the hard bank, until he is exhausted. His head is bloodied and grotesque like the dead slave's head at his feet. He dimly knows he cannot escape; he dimly knows he does not wish to go back to prison. He feels tired, tired of being a coward, of capitulating, tired of trying to get his father's love, of pleasing those he hates, tired of swaggering and boasting, tired of being someone he is not.

He no longer feels, he no longer thinks; he is in a stupor. He crawls along the ground on his belly toward the river. He slides into the water effortlessly; he continues sliding as though entering a familiar and welcome place, a place where he can rest comfortably, without any care: the river's womb. He drowns.

Dear little Sphinx, you do have courage. You had tremendous courage and sensitivity to care so much for the slave you killed. It was your destiny in that life to find courage, even though you found no other way than to take your own life.

I have learned about the depth of your feelings, I have experienced your defenses, I have learned that those defenses are not rigidly imprinted in you. You are a delicate soul, as my papa was, as the young teacher was, as the old scientist was, and as my true male is. I know courage and assertion are within you. I will look for these qualities within me and I will bring them out of me.

Papa, you will no longer be my male self. I will use your sensitivity, your gentleness, your creativity, but I will discard your cowardice, sadism, and lack of assertion. I can understand now why I have not been more assertive. My male selves have been punished, tormented, tortured, and perhaps even crucified for being themselves. I suppose we all must endure such lives in the process of finding the kernel of our real being. But at what point do we learn to live from that Self and never betray it, no matter what?

As life unfolds,
the soul clamors
to be heard.
It says,
"You are not they.
You are a larger being.
Take the veils from your
eyes.
Listen to the small,
small voice within.
Let it guide you to your
Self.

The soul —
the watcher —

the keeper —
hovers around you
like a moonbeam.
It shines on your frame,
bringing truth

within.

This guardian angel —
this monitoring force —
moves steadfastly
in your being.
Call upon it —
invite it in —
listen to its
enlightened voice.

It is your friend.
It is WHO YOU ARE.

The rest must be looked at
AND TRANSMUTED."

Looked at and transmuted. Looked at and transmuted.
But first, a little rest, soul. A little reprieve,
so I can sleep on this information. I want to let it
swim inside me, connecting, discovering, clarifying.
All in all, I want to make peace with it.

Time! It will take time —
Not much; a little.
Ah, yes, these are the places where the morsels fit.
They blend with my consciousness of today.

Yes, now I understand —
more of me.

You were a coward, male self, even then.
Female self, you were a despot.
Rectify.
Find the courage to live life differently.
You know the outcome of those qualities from
centuries past.
Do not repeat them; rectify.
Bring strength and honor to both energies.
Even though you are still afraid of stonings, crucifixion,
torture,
ride like a valiant warrior on your white steed,
Pegasus:
Pegasus the energy of Spirit.
Conquer those energies.
Become connected to a stronger male and female self,
to God,
the deity from which you have sprung.

Move forward, accept these pieces,
be grateful for the consciousness
they give your psyche.

With a long breath, I said:
"Yes!"
I said to my feminine energy:
"I'm ready for more."

34

A Habit of Deadly Superiority

In a convent:

> My soul wished to atone
> for the despot's evil,
> to make amends for
> the vengeance within me.
> I lived a life of prayer and
> supplication.
> I gained insight into my
> true nature:
>
> I was strong and principled,
> yet delicate.
>
> I oversaw my sisters.
> I bestowed love upon them.
> They reciprocated —
> with their love.
>
> I thrived in this atmosphere,
> glowing,

with the conviction that
I had been redeemed.

I was known to those around me
to be young and beautiful,
to love beauty, laughter, and God.
A priest from whom I took lessons
became captivated by my charm.
He could not contain his love.

His prayers to his angels
were of no avail.
He broke the rules to be near me.
They caught him standing at
my window at night,
instead of
staying in the monastery.

I was aware of this man's torment.
I was flattered as much as annoyed.
There lurked in my psyche
a desire for his punishment.
It was a mystery to me,
whence such thirst for
vengeance came.

Had I not made a vow
for a celestial nuptial?
What right had he to interfere?
I am chaste,
I am innocent.
How dare he invade my sanctity?
I spurned him
in disdain.

There emerged from my psyche
a hidden venom.
I pretended not to feel it.
Instead,
I requested punishment
for his offensive behavior.
"He should be cast
out of the church."

The authorities listened.
They exiled him.
It made a great stir.
I was exalted by the others,
for my pure, intense
devotion to God.

I became exalted more
than ever.
My name —
a household word,
an example.
I was deified, glorified —

I almost believed
in my own glory.

I wanted to believe it,
but the doubts stirred
inside me.
My hidden guilt was
playing tricks on me —
"Was the people's
adoration wrong?"

But, eventually,
I succumbed.

I finished my life
in the convent.
I never forgot the face
of the priest
whom I had helped to
dishonor.

I died —
wondering about
my vengeance —

asking —
God
for
forgiveness.

I had indeed rectified
my wrathful nature,
atoned for the misdeeds
of the other life.

I left this life —
wondering —
"Why can I not
surrender?
Why is my heart
hardened
to
the
man?"

As the Mother Superior, a loving, giving, beautiful self. Also, however, once again, my ancient resolve never to surrender to a man. What is needed to heal this wound?

You need to claim your male energy, Anneliese, and to surrender to your true female energy so the two will be in balance. And the only way is through forgiveness.

35

The Spirit of Forgiveness

I sat in the morning hour, in the quiet of my room, meditating on the word "forgiveness."

> What came into view was a heavenly world.
> I saw it as clearly as my Earth domain.
> I became suffused with an ecstasy.
> It took me to an elevated state.
>
> Approaching me were three wise old men.
> Their beards were white.
> They brought me gently to a table,
> where they conversed with me.
>
> There was no speech.
> It was not necessary.
> Thoughts were conveyed through
> their entire being.
> It was a language
> I could understand —
> communication on the highest level.

Into my mind flashed many scenes:
those of lives I had lived before,
tortured lives,
innocent lives,
and lives of atonement.

I saw the life of a vengeful monarch,
at a time when I had been
exceedingly cruel
to a young beautiful maiden —
the daughter of my
lady-in-waiting.

I had punished this young woman brutally,
more brutally because not only was she
beautiful,
but also because her wisdom was admired by all.
I, the monarch, disfigured
her body and mind.
I then banished her from the kingdom.

The sages beckoned to me
to behold this maiden,
to look deeply upon her countenance.
I fell back in bewilderment
and disbelief —

I recognized the face —
of
my
mother!

I collapsed onto the table before me.
I banged my fists upon it.

I screamed to them:
"No!
This is not so.
No!
I will not believe this vision.

"It is she who has been vengeful to me.
I was the victim,
not she!
She was the instigator of my sorrow.
I cannot forgive her.
I will not believe this."

The wise men answered:

"The scales will remain askew
until you desire to change the patterns
of victimization and revenge.
Your viciousness then
evoked her retaliation.
Your victimization now
brings forth her revenge."

I was silent, my body still.
When I looked again upon their holy faces,
I felt disfigured,
my countenance stained
by the truth of their statements.

They beckoned me
to look into the distance.
They produced before me the image
of a house for the insane.
In it was the figure of a man.

I recognized the slave
I had loved so devotedly
while in a tribe of women.

I recoiled with loathing from this vision.
I buried my head in my hands.
"Oh, Masters, must you be cruel?
Must you torture me
with these ancient tales?"

They conveyed to me that
now was the moment,
the moment of rectification
and redemption,
I must look at the man before me
and remember our trials together.

I looked and remembered
how he had betrayed me —
telling the queen he knew me not,
while her henchmen performed
their butchery,
and I lay stunned and bleeding.

I remembered how,
as I lay before them dying,
I had cursed men,
had vowed revenge —
never, ever to surrender —
but to destroy them all.

Thereafter,
all men were to be
used for sex.

I rebuked them
when they wanted me.
I scorned their desires.
I played viciously
with their nature —
until one of them,
broken by my taunting,
was taken away —
his mind deranged.

The wise men said:

"Look well upon this man's
distorted face.
Look deep into his eyes."

I pulled away.
The sages insisted.
I was shocked to see
that instead of blame
his eyes were pleading
for forgiveness.

I heard the witless man's
inner cry.
He had betrayed me long ago.
He had betrayed me
in this life as well,
when he had shoved me,
his child, into that cellar.

I looked at the wise men
utterly perplexed.
"Can this be so?" I asked.

"Was I this man's daughter
in this life?
Was he also one I had spurned?"

The wise ones answered:

"After your death in the tribal life,
and after many other lives,
you met again.
You drove him mad.
He had wanted to love you —
to atone for his former cowardice.
Your vengeance destroyed him.

"Again you met.
This time you were a child.
But he could not return your love —
still passive —
dominated by the queen bee —
your
mother.

"In this life, as formerly,
he has been a coward —
too weak to give his love —
either to the little girl you were
or the woman
he loved and betrayed."

I looked again into his eyes,
eyes begging for release
from the torturous guilt
his cowardice had produced —

eyes begging for his soul
to be redeemed.

I looked upon him
in wonderment.
I pondered the awesome
wheel of destiny.
Life was indeed a miraculous journey —
a drama
of rectification and redemption.

I touched his face with a gentleness —
a gentleness that made him cry.
I also cried.
We forgave one another —
bringing to an end
a monstrous cycle.

The wise men showed me once again
the image of the woman
I had recognized as my mother.
She also looked at me
with pleading eyes,
asking for forgiveness.

She knelt before me
repenting her misdeeds.
I picked her up and held her.
I asked for forgiveness
for the brutality I had
inflicted
when she was the daughter
of my lady-in-waiting.

I touched her face.
She smiled with gratitude.
I held her close to my heart.
Her image disappeared into the
atmosphere —

I was left with my own
female
self.

I felt the joy of my own
sweet nature,
of my gentleness, warmth,
and strength.
I sensed my stature —
that of a giantess.
I was my true woman —
at last.

Forgiveness had brought
a radiance to my being.
I was luminous.
The wise men disappeared.
The images of my parents had been
transmuted.

I was on the path to
my "I am."

The ancient resolve for pain
was broken forever.
Removed from my psyche.
The balance was achieved.
My hungry soul requited.

God!
Thy Will be done —
Not mine
alone.

36

The Anatomy of Forgiveness

The poet Rumi wrote a poem in which he asks the eyes, the heart and the liver to speak to him. When they do, he receives from these contact points important information which he uses poetically. I was inspired by this poem to create an "imaging" exercise.

Through this imaging process, I would get in touch with the liver, the organ of assimilation; then the cerebellum, the organ of equilibrium and balance; and, finally, the cerebrum, the organ of memory and intelligence, according to esoteric literature. They helped me in my endeavor to forgive.

Your mother has long since incarnated. It is good that you wish to forgive her. Her deeds have been engraved in your psyche, but since you recognize they were your deeds as well, you can henceforth forgive her and by doing so forgive yourself, freeing you from your own bondage.

See yourself as you truly are: strong, beautiful, noble, receptive, loving and creative. You have rectified your misdeeds in lives of the past and in this life. Recognize who you truly are! When you are in touch with your real and true identity, you will wish to discard negative imagery.

Remember, it was when you refused to understand that you were a reflection of her that you remained allied with her in hatred and victimization.

I understood how necessary it was for me to live from my true qualities, at the same time continuing to rectify the residues of my old selves. I understood I had much to do in this life. I had been told it would be a life of constant discovery of my real self, from which I would teach others. My terror of being was at an end. I would no longer fear surrendering to a man, for I was indeed beginning to be connected to my true female self.

At the end of my meditation I was told to take to the liver, the organ of assimilation, the information I had been given. The liver instructed me to bring this imagery throughout my body — which gave me a sense of wholeness.

I sat quietly for a while, absorbing what I had learned. I then rose to my feet and, with my left side, moved in space with a soft, round movement of my arm and body, which reached out to the world and brought back to me what I found. I repeated these movements, swaying my hips while my arms continued to make gestures of giving and receiving. I then raised both arms above my head and brought them, palms facing each other, to my solar plexus. The tears streamed from my eyes as I affirmed myself softly: "I feel so beautiful, so angelic, so much me. I am a beautiful woman. Thank you, God. Thank you."

Only now did I begin to realize that the male was also a human being, with the same feelings as the female. He was also desirous of loving and being loved; he was vulnerable and sensitive; he could be kind, wise, creative, and assertive without being harmful.

I put my hand on my liver and told it that I wanted to forgive my papa. The liver instructed me to go to the cerebellum for permission to do this. When permission was granted, I returned to the liver and asked for help from the cerebrum. In this enlightened place, the imagery of my weak papa was quickly and cleanly separated from me, wafted away, and replaced by a strong, straight, direct male image. He was sensitive, sure, and vitally energized. He wanted to fulfill his mission in this life and wanted to do so without hesitation.

I beamed with pride and delight as I brought his image into focus, receiving permission from the liver to let it permeate my body. Without hesitation I moved the right side of my body with a strength and a force that were beautiful to behold. As I moved around the room, I was reminded of the Masai warriors I had seen in Africa. These warriors stood straight as spears — prideful, handsome and valorous. I understood I wanted to make my way in the world, to contribute to it and leave my mark upon it.

The discarded male and female energies of my mother and father, as well as my unwanted selves, were almost discernible energies in the room.

In accordance with Jesus' parable, I jubilantly envisioned gathering up the tares, binding them and burning them in the fire. I ritualized the transformation of these old energies by concentrating on burning them in a gigantic fire, until they disappeared into ashes.

Then, in accordance with the parable, which speaks of gathering the wheat into the barns, I looked into the ashes. Out of the ashes rose a new male and female, synchronized, growing taller and taller, as they merged with the heavens. At last.

37

An Angel in Residence

What would it be like
if my male and female
were in balance?
The archangel in my being
would radiate.
My wingspan would encompass
the width, the length, the height,
the depth
of the universe.

This is the dimension
of my soul —
my essence —
so near to God.

I have struggled against the
voices of disbelief,
jeering
that I, a witless
"not I" being —
eternally seeking

a balanced male and female state,
should have in residence
an angel.

This angel has plagued me
into listening —
teaching me to repel
the voices of my overzealous brain,
denying all
but their own garbled screams,
drowning out the
angel's songs.

One day,
I stopped listening
to my earthly self,
enveloped in its corporeal
"I."
I pushed beyond the egoed frame,
melting willingly
into my
"I am."

I now stand tall —
eye-to-eye with the mountaintops,
looking down at my feet,
walking on the earth —
treading gently
so as not to step
on any living form.

I caress these forms.
I bring them lovingly
into my hands.

I converse with them.
My fellow humans feel
my giant's glimpse of life —
a draught of consciousness
offered to their thirsting souls
which they in turn
impart to others.

What would it be like
if my male and female
were in balance?

My intrinsic Self
so close to God
would then take form:

An archangel
residing
on
the
earth.

Guide to Terms
Used in This Book

Bioenergetics. "A therapeutic technique to help a person get back together with his body and to help him enjoy to the fullest degree possible the life of the body. This emphasis on the body includes sexuality . . . as well as breathing, moving, feeling and self-expression." (*Bioenergetics*, Alexander Lowen, M.D., p. 43, Coward, McCann & Geoghegan, Inc., NY 1975.) This therapeutic modality was founded by Dr. Alexander Lowen and Dr. John Pierrakos.

Breathing Stool. A therapeutic tool devised by Drs. Lowen and Pierrakos to help the patient elicit breathing. It is two feet in height. Rolled blankets secured by cords are placed on it. The patient arches face-up over the stool, feet grounded under the legs. This stress position will elicit breathing. The patient's capacity or incapacity to breathe gives the therapist information about the "armoring" of the patient's body.

Armoring. A term coined by Wilhelm Reich, founder of Vegeto-therapy, the root of Bioenergetics. Armoring refers to the muscular tension in the body that provides a shield against painful and threatening emotional experiences. The organism can begin its armoring from the time of birth, if not before.

Use of Tennis Racket. The racket is held in both hands and the arms are stretched behind the shoulders, head, and body. The body is thus in an arched position, coming from grounded legs and feet. When it is in this position for a period of time, breathing is elicited, particularly when the mouth is ajar. The entire body becomes activated. The racket is used to hit a bed that is customarily present in the therapist's office for this purpose.

Hitting the bed from this arched position is used to express the rage the person is contending with.

Symbiosis. The paralyzed emotional state of two people who cannot separate themselves from each other because they have pasted images of their parents onto the other. In such a state, neither person lives from himself/herself. This superimposed state serves to keep the psyche alive, since living through another gives the person an identity.

Transference. An important psychological tool by which the patient transfers his/her feelings onto the therapist. In my case I made a god out of Dr. Warner. This was an intensified reaction to not having had adequate nurturing from my own father. This projection must be worked through. With a skillful therapist, such a projection can be worked with so, in time, the patient will be able to differentiate between the therapist and the parent.

Counter Transference. The conscious or unconscious reaction of the therapist to the patient. This reaction must be worked through in order for the patient to be seen objectively by the therapist. Only then can the patient can gain freedom to move forward in life.

Reflectivism. The belief that in a noncoincidental universe, qualities from your past existences purposefully occur in your parents, to be "reflected" once more in you. By being the object of actions you once imposed upon others, you can face, accept, and surmount your own limitations. It is a concept of self-responsibility and self-absolution.

Exercise for Forgiveness. In asking for forgiveness from my mother, I placed my right hand on my liver, asking it what I needed to do to forgive her. The liver responded by telling me to get permission from my the cerebellum. The cerebellum gave this permission. The thoughts that I heard were as follows: "Even though it is difficult for you to forgive her, you must do so in order to move from victimization to a truer state."

I then went to the cerebrum, the organ of equilibrium and balance, and heard the following: "Your mother has long since incarnated. It is good that you wish to forgive her. Her deeds have been engraved in your psyche, but since you recognize they were your deeds as well, you can forgive her; by doing so, you are enabled to forgive yourself, freeing you from further karma. See yourself as you truly are: strong, beautiful, noble, receptive, loving, and creative. You have rectified your misdeeds in lives of the past and in this life. Now, live fully."

Activating the New Image. When the above information has been incorporated, I suggest that the female patient express, through movement of her body, the feminine aspect of her nature. This can also be done with her male energy. When both the female and male energies have been cleansed, I propose to my clients that they have a dialogue between the two energies. This will usually lead to a union of the new energies, which, in their purity, join with the intrinsic nature of the person's Godself. The same exercise can be used with a male patient.